The Chieftain's Daughter

'One of the most powerful examples of Irish children's historical fiction ... Subtly conveyed sense of time and place, searingly vivid characters ...'

Robert Dunbar, *Children's Books In Ireland*

'From the very first sentence we know we are in the presence of an expert storyteller. A complex and moving story.'

The Irish Times

'One of the best and most perceptive writers for young people.'
The Guardian

'Sam McBratney writes with a refreshingly individual style; his characters, both children and adult, are clear and convincing.'
Times Literary Supplement

'The characters are so real that even when you put the book down, you find yourself still living in the fifth century.'
Woman's Way

SAM MCBRATNEY

SAM MCBRATNEY lives in County Antrim and is the author of numerous books for children and young adults, including *The Green Kids* and *Art, You're Magic* and the internationally renowned *Guess How Much I Love You?*. He won the Bisto Award for *Put a Saddle on the Pig* (now called *You Just Don't Listen*) and also received the Bass Ireland Arts Prize. He is married, with three grown-up children. He also has an ancient tortoise!

THE CHIEFTAIN'S DAUGHTER

SAM McBRATNEY

THE O'BRIEN PRESS
DUBLIN

First published 1993 by The O'Brien Press Ltd.,
20 Victoria Road, Dublin 6, Ireland.
Tel: +353 1 4923333; Fax: +353 1 4922777
E-mail: books@obrien.ie
Website: www.obrien.ie
Reprinted 1994, 2001.

ISBN 0-86278-338-0

British Library Cataloguing-in-Publication Data
McBratney Sam
Chieftain's Daughter
I. Title II. White, Kate
823.914 [J]

3 4 5 6 7 8 9
01 02 03 04 05

The O'Brien Press receives
assistance from

Section drawings: Katharine White
Editing, typesetting, design and layout: The O'Brien Press Ltd.
Colour separations: C&A Print Services Ltd.
Printing: Cox & Wyman Ltd.

Contents

PROLOGUE

A part from the smile that he wore, the stranger was unarmed. As the old chief, Dinn Keene, watched him come into the village he could see that this was not a man to be feared in the ordinary way. No doubt it was the same in every village he came into, and parents with their children whispered his name as they crowded round – Patrick of the Pens, the great Man of Speech.

Yes, thought Dinn Keene. Approaching his hut was a man of presence, a visitor to stop even the anvil ringing while he passed. The dogs, though, yelped to be up and at his throat. To a dog, a stranger is a stranger.

'My name is Patrick.'

Dinn Keene nodded once.

'My three companions are waiting at your gates with the horses – we have travelled in peace and friendship to speak with Dinn Keene and the people of the village. We would like to stay with you for a few days if this is possible.'

With spreading hands, the old chief invited the stranger to sit with him in the open air. There was less smoke out here, and more light.

'Let your companions come forward,' said Dinn Keene, 'the horses will be cared for. The food you see coming is a kind of stew. It's a bit on the thin side for my liking, but try it.'

The stranger said that he was most grateful, then closed his eyes and spoke some further words of thanks to a person he called Heavenly Father.

'And when you have eaten,' Dinn Keene added quietly, 'I would like you and your companions to travel on from here.'

After a careful pause, the stranger said, 'Of course. But I wonder why – when powerful princes of the plains have gladly given me right of way and freedom to preach – why not Dinn Keene? Perhaps you don't know who I am?'

'You are a man of speech who tells stories about Mary's Great Son. You sit down with important people in this land and across the sea. I know you.'

'But not with Dinn Keene? You have nothing to fear from the things I say, it is only the Truth.'

Only the truth, thought the old man. Now there was a weapon to carry round with you! It would test the best of armour or the deepest ditch.

'They tell me you are a great sayer, Patrick of the Pens. What are you like at listening? You see, I have been expecting you for many years now – or somebody very like you. I knew that you would walk into my village one day and sit down there and tell me your version of the truth over a bowl of food. Actually, you've come a little late in the day.'

A glance from the stranger. 'I don't understand.'

'You will understand. I want to explain as well as I can why there is nothing for you here. You may rest a while and leave after the noon, hopefully with some sun on your back, and find another village to speak in.'

The stranger blew on a full spoon, to cool his stew. 'You have me curious. I am listening.'

PART ONE

THE ROUND OF STONES

CHAPTER 1

As you can see to look at me (said Old Dinn Keene) I have been given a fair number of years by the spirits I believe in. Of course, you will know that these are the ancient spirits of my people, not the God-all-Father that you have come to tell me about.

The first time in my life when I can remember feeling broken inside happened when I was eight years old, or maybe it was nine or more – who bothers to keep count of the years? My mother came to my bed-couch one morning and shook me awake.

'Dinn Keene,' she said, 'waken up now and put on your clothes, you have to go away.'

And before I could rub the sleep from my eyes, they had dressed me. Only now did I notice the worry in my mother's face, and Corag Mor standing behind her, fully clothed.

'Where am I going?'

'Away. It's quite far, so hurry yourself.'

'And you?'

'Don't be silly, Dinn Keene, *I* can't go. But when it's safe ... when it's safe we'll come and get you.'

I glanced up at Corag Mor, already wrapped up in his cloak for the journey. He was a tall and impressive man. As one of our priests he had great influence over my mother, but I did not like him even a little bit. I had seen him with the blood of twitching cocks dripping from his elbows. Was I being sent away with the man who made sacrifices?

'I'm not going.'

'You're going. You have to go. Your father is fighting with his enemies and it's going to be very dangerous here, so let there be no nonsense or he will beat you with the flat of his sword.' She clutched me in her arms, and said, 'Oh be brave, my wee one!'

Then she released me to fetch some porridge from the fire. When I had eaten, my mother carried me outside in a green blanket to where Corag Mor waited on a huge grey horse.

'At least you'll have your sucking blanket,' she whispered foolishly, and then between them they bundled me on board. I remember that my mother stood at the horse's head and held on to one of my feet for a little while.

'Make sure you take good care of him.'

'I know these people,' said Corag Mor. 'He will be safe there.'

With that, he dug in his heels and set us galloping across the Plain of Meath with little Dinn Keene slithering about the neck of the horse. After a time, Corag Mor stopped riding so that he could tie a cord round both of us. The rhythm of the horse, the heat of it below me and of Corag Mor behind, must have made me sleep, for the day passed quickly enough. Towards evening we dismounted in a copse of thorns to avoid a band of mounted warriors. Shortly before darkness, in the time we call the wolf-light, Corag Mor found us a sheltered place at the edge of a great gloomy wood.

I, Dinn Keene, felt that I was lost. The trees all round rustled like a living thing. I was accustomed to walls about me in the night, and the knowledge that my father slept close by with a sword stuffed down the straw of his bed. Why then was I here in this wild place with a man who couldn't even be bothered to talk to me?

'You needn't cry, boy, there's no point in it,' he said to me, a hunched figure in the wolf-light.

I blamed my mother for sending me away. I cannot recall her face, since I never saw her again, but Corag Mor's has stayed in my mind. His beard was square-cut, like a spade, and worn without a moustache – the rare fashion of one who always liked to mark himself out from the crowd. I can still see that tangle of red-bronze hair; that hooked nose which lorded it over his face; that face which was always on guard in case his lips were surprised by that warm, too-human thing called a smile. I think I never heard him laugh.

I wakened in the morning with his hand over my mouth.

'Not a sound!' he hissed at me.

This was the only hint of the danger we were in. I had no idea why he suddenly ran to the fringe of the wood, or why the horse shuffled so uneasily on her toes. Then I saw the shapes flitting among the trees and terror came into my body with such a spurt that I shouted out, 'Wolves!'

In truth, they were worse than wolves. Some fine prince's pack of hunting dogs, now run wild, had come upon us. Even as I watched, one of the beasts broke cover and studied the knife in Corag Mor's hand with horrifying patience and contempt.

In a dreadful hurry now, Corag Mor ran towards me, and for a moment I did not know whether to be more terrified of his knife than of the dogs. But he ran right by, seized the horse by the neck and drove his knife into the animal from underneath. In this way he brought the shuddering mare to her knees.

'Come with me, Dinn Keene. Slowly, now. The brutes are starving, all they want is food. The horse will do for them.'

'But I don't want them to eat the horse.'

'There are many horses, only one Dinn Keene.'

So saying, he grabbed me, and put me round his neck.

'Look ahead, Dinn Keene – do you see the mountain? It's called the Grey Man because his head is in the clouds and his feet are in the sea. Soon we'll be there.'

'I don't want to go there!'

'Hold still, and I'll tell you the story of Balor's bad pig.'

At last, without further alarms, we reached the place which Corag Mor called the high lake. This was a bowl of bright water whose surface was roughened by the same steady wind that bent the reeds and howled in my hood. Here and there small islands broke the water like the humps of a serpent's back.

Dinn Keene said, 'I'm hungry.'

'That's where the Lake-dwellers have their island,' said Corag Mor, ignoring me. 'Where we are going is not far. Long ago, when I was your age, this was my country.' And he breathed in deeply, as if the air was sweet.

Once again I stepped into Corag Mor's shadow to follow him down a path which took us presently into more agreeable country. At one point the ground fell away from us into a lush, green hollow where wild fruit grew. I was ready to launch myself at it, but Corag Mor held me fast.

'Go carefully.' His voice was soft. 'This is a special place, we are not alone here.'

I, Dinn Keene, looked and saw no-one. A tall rowan tree grew out of the hollow to the level of our eyes, and on its branches, fluttering like unearthly fruits, were ribbons of cloth. And on the grassy floor of the hollow I saw a large circle of self-standing stones.

'Are we going down there?' I asked.

'Come on.' Corag Mor took my hand. 'And be sure you do what I do when we get there.'

The priest, I remember, stood very still at the centre of the Round, and the expression on his face was that of someone who is trying to hear whether it is raining outside. Each stone in the circle was taller than my head, and deeply embedded in a circular bank like an old hound's tooth. As I wandered among them, Corag Mor suddenly grabbed my arm with such force that I winced with pain.

'Move to your right! You must always walk the circle sunwise-round.'

'Why?'

'Because it pleases the spirits who live here.'

'Who are the spirits?'

'It is not good to mention their names, just do as you're told. One day you'll understand. Maybe. It's only a few people who know the power there is in a place like this.'

'Are you one of them?'

'Aye, I'm one of them.'

Perhaps it is true that Corag Mor heard the spirits and felt their presence, I do not know. I am certain, however, that he, too, had his version of the Truth, for he became excited and alive each time he ventured into that ancient Round. Perhaps his spirit is still there. He died in that very place some years later.

'What am I going to do with him!' Chief Ruadh demanded to be told. 'I have a son already, and three daughters, where am I going to put him? And how long is he here for? It's true that I'm glad to see you, Corag Mor, but you're my brother. I'm sorry, but I can't be pleased that you've brought me another mouth to feed. No, no, I'm not well pleased!'

This was the welcome which Dinn Keene received at journey's end. We sat in the open, round a fire of wood and peat which threw off violent twists of smoke. The mountain men didn't seem to mind having their heads in the stinking fumes.

'You have no choice, Ruadh,' said Corag Mor calmly. 'You are the boy's fostering-father.'

'Am I? I swear by the hair on that dog's tail, Corag Mor, I don't like being told who my children are.'

'It's an honour, believe me.'

'Huh!'

Chief Ruadh gathered in his short legs in disgust. He wore a badger-skin coat and he sat in a willow-cane chair that creaked when he moved. To little Dinn Keene he seemed more like an apparition than a real person. But my heart soared with hope when I heard how he refused me! I did not want to spend a single night in one of their four, crude huts. Surely now, Corag Mor would have to take me home again?

Corag Mor reached into the folds of his cloak and produced a bronze-headed weapon with a double edge. It was a splendid axe, finely worked – but Dinn Keene had seen many of these, he could not understand why the sight of it should bring gasps of wonder from the strangers round the fire.

'Life is different on the plains, Ruadh,' said Corag Mor. 'The boy's father is a warrior-chief and he has men to command, all with weapons like these and horses standing under them. You should be grateful he does not come into the mountains and take tribute from you.'

'What tribute?' cried Ruadh. 'There's nothing for him here, he would return to the plains empty-handed and with skinnier horses. Did he ... send me this axe?'

'Yes. A gift. To show his goodwill.'

Ruadh ran his thumb along one of the edges. His eyebrows twitched, thick as corn-sheaves. Then he snatched his own axe from his belt and tossed it towards a boy of my own size. To my astonishment I saw that it was nothing more than a piece of stone tied to a wooden handle. Then he turned to me, and closed his fingers around Dinn Keene's jaw.

'Now hear this, boy. You will cut wood, fetch water, bury bad smells, mind goats in your turn and always behave yourself like all good natural-born sons of mine should behave themselves. And if you don't, I will hold you up by the heels and give you a real good dusting. You'll act like you're one of us. Yes?'

Little Dinn Keene's eyes watered, partly because of the woodsmoke that would not leave him alone, and partly because he was thinking of his mother and the people who loved him.

How long would I be lost among these strangers who made axes out of stones, who lived on Grey Man Mountain in the clouds?

CHAPTER 2

I, Dinn Keene, stayed on Grey Man Mountain for not less than five years and not more than seven. I quickly forgot my mother's face and the comfort of my father's sturdy dwelling on the far plains. Instead I had the new-found companionship of Chief Ruadh's hut.

There were no such things as rooms in Ruadh's hut, no private places, no partitions. The fire belched smoke in the middle of the floor. Seven people slept there with two hairy hounds that growled if you took their place, and on the coldest nights goats were admitted also.

Ruadh himself was a powerful, stubby man, so proud of his badger coat that he rarely left it off his back. When he drank crab-apple wine he got down on all fours and bit the dogs. It was Ruadh who taught me how to cast a sling, stalk deer, land fish and braid hair. His own hair, like Corag Mor's, was the colour of the leaves that winter on the trees. I loved him. He used to say that when my real father came to take me back, he was going to give him someone else – one of the bad, good-for-nothing children of the camp. This was a great game. The children used to run away from him, screaming, 'No, not me, not me!'

Everyone there was important to me. I could easily say much about old Breasal, who said songs; Eithne who was in charge of marrow bones; the fearsome Bodman Tar; young Ennis the archer; my friend Oscar. But I must speak now of my lovely Frann.

She was Ard Bruill's daughter. Somehow her memory has stayed fresh with me. I can fairly give her a spray of fine hair the colour of hay, but with more lustre. Often she wove a sprig of heather into her braids, and thus decorated, would come away with Oscar and me to hang upside down from the branches of trees. I did not like Oscar to look at her too closely. I used to poke him with the butt end of my spear for looking too closely.

I remember that Frann had a roving curiosity about all things. On our way to fish or fetch water she would suddenly stop, and call us over to examine something like a trail of slug-slime or a curtain of ice in the depths of a hedge. She was a lithe and eager creature when we played chasing games, and how it made her miserable to lose! She had scars on both knees and was skilled with the sling.

Such was Frann. I came to understand that she had eyes in the back of her head, for she would whip round suddenly, and say, 'Who do *you* think you're looking at, Dinn Keene?'

I had been in the mountains two or three years when I realised that I must do something about this girl who was always in my thoughts. In some way I had to establish that I was her special friend – certainly more special than Oscar, whom I thought of as a great rival. But what could I do? I had neither the words for my vague feelings nor the courage to make them completely public. Some action was called for to make me significant – certainly more significant than Oscar!

One night, lying with my back to one of the goats, I had the idea. I will give her my green sucking blanket, thought Dinn Keene.

This is what happened.

Dinn Keene waited patiently until one morning Breasal came to the door of her hut and called out to Frann, 'Here, take this pot and get me some nettle-heads.'

'Me?' said Frann, who was fondling the ears of her spoiled dog. I was jealous of the beast, and wished I had ears like him.

'Well, I'm not talking to the *dog*,' said Breasal.

'I'll get stung.'

'You'll get stung if you don't, my girl!'

Dinn Keene followed her. The blanket was under his arm, rolled up in a rush mat. He stalked her as if she were a wild beast, and his heart pounded so much that he trembled at the edges of his body.

And then, in the glade which is known as Ulmar's Great Snare, she heard him behind her, and turned.

'What are you doing there, Dinn Keene?'

'I was trying to catch up with you.'

'You were sneaking up on me.'

'I wasn't sneaking up on you, I want to give you something. Here.'

Dinn Keene saw at once that he had surprised her with his generosity. As she took the rush mat and spilled the contents to the ground, her eyelids flickered in wonder. Of course, the blanket was no longer in perfect order, but still, it was far superior to anything that Eithne could produce by her simple weaving.

'Why are you giving me this?' she asked.

Because it is my only possession, thought Dinn Keene. Because I have guarded it tooth and nail against dogs and goats and people since I came to this place.

'I don't really want it any more.'

'But it's your sucking blanket.'

'It's not my sucking blanket.'

'It is so.'

'I don't suck blankets!' cried Dinn Keene in a rage.

'Well, Oscar says you do. You *used* to.'

At that moment Dinn Keene would have split Oscar like a block of wood had he ventured into the clearing. It was true that he used to fall asleep in Ruadh's tent with a corner of the blanket in his mouth – but only in the beginning, for a little while, until the strangeness wore off him.

'Right!' he said hotly. 'Don't have it, then. I'll take it back and give it to somebody else. Eithne's baby can have it.'

'No,' said Frann, pouncing on the blanket, 'I'll have it. Thank you, Dinn Keene. I have to go now, Breasal wants nettles for soup.'

Dinn Keene wandered home that day as if he had sprouted feathers. Somewhere in the glen his Frann was picking nettle heads with his blanket round her shoulders like a shawl. He had showed himself to be a very generous person – certainly more generous than Oscar – and the whole affair made him feel good and worthy of being loved.

Until the following day. Dinn Keene returned to the village with water and soon sensed that something was different. Bodman Tar winked at him, and grinned. He was not the only one. Other people smiled in the same mysterious way, and sly Oscar pretended to whistle while watching like a hawk out of one eye.

Now there was in the village a murderous, slobbering beast called Halfwolf. Murta, who looked after it, kept it tethered to a post during the day, away from people, so that the creature would not be spoiled like the other dogs by too much fondling, and only let it go to roam the glens by night. Dinn Keene could not fail to notice that Halfwolf had acquired a new bed. The beast was curled up nose to tail on the green blanket.

The glee on Oscar's face, and the innocence on Frann's, was too much for Dinn Keene. Seizing the nearest useful object, which happened to be a pole, he tried to shift the creature and rake the blanket clear. The hound came out of its doze with a venomous snarl, gripped the pole with its teeth, and shook poor Dinn Keene at the other end from head to foot.

When Dinn Keene saw that he could not even get the pole back, he said to himself: Dinn Keene, you have lost your blanket.

He had lost much more. Bodman Tar sat some way off with a knowing smile on his face, and Murta bowed his head to snigger in his chest. These, and many more, had a good laugh at his red face.

Oscar knew that he wasn't safe when he saw Dinn Keene coming, and took off like a hare. But Frann did not flinch.

'You gave my blanket to that dog.'

'Oscar dared me to.'

'And you did it!'

'Yes, it was mine, you gave it to me because you didn't want it and anyway you can always suck your thumb if you're stuck for something to suck.'

There was only one answer for such a mouthful. His fist smacked into her face, smashing her to the ground.

'It was the only thing I had. It was my only thing!' he screeched at her, lying there propped on one elbow, staring up at him with shock in her eyes and blood oozing from her bottom lip.

'I hate you, Dinn Keene,' she said.

Let her hate me, thought Dinn Keene! He took pleasure from the very strength of her feeling, for he was the cause of it. In a way it made him significant – certainly more significant than Oscar, who at this moment was hiding among the blackberry brakes.

But I must speak to you now (said old Dinn Keene) of Corag Mor. He, too, was a person of great importance in my story.

You will understand that the people of Chief Ruadh's clan, though not humble by nature, well knew that there are powers in this world who are greater than men or armies of men. For this reason they were glad that Corag Mor had returned to them. He understood the ways of the Otherworld better than they did.

Corag Mor took to painting his face. To come upon him suddenly in the wolf-light, gaudy as a poison berry from the neck up, put more fear into me than a real spirit would have done. From time to time he laid an offering in the Round of Stones. He had the power to go on a journey – that is, to sit in the same place without moving while his mind left him. We all shuddered to think what he might be looking at.

One evening a blue flame appeared in the fire. Ruadh, who was a little drunk, called for Corag Mor to examine it.

'There it is! See? What's it doing there? Why is the little devil burning blue?'

'It's probably a drop of fat from the hen you ate,' said Breasal.

'Hen's fat doesn't burn blue. Murta, have you ever seen hen's fat burn blue?'

Murta, after a wink at his wife, replied solemnly. 'I have seen many things in my time, but never that. I've never seen hen's fat burn blue. How about you, Ennis?'

'No,' said Ennis. 'I've seen a pig's fat burn purple, but never blue.'

'There's a reason for everything, you know,' Ruadh said after draining his cup. 'Everything has a reason. Well, Corag Mor? Explain the blue flame.'

'It may be a warning.'

'A warning? Of what?'

'I don't know.'

'How do you know it's a warning, then? It might be anything.'

'The flame is unnatural,' said Corag Mor, 'so there must be an unnatural reason for it. What that reason is ... Who knows?'

'It's hungry,' cried Ruadh, suddenly raising his voice. 'Frann, come here, girl, bring me what's left of the pig lard, this poor fire is hungry.'

'Don't you dare throw good food on that fire!' shouted Breasal.

As Ruadh brightened the fire with the pig lard, I watched what Frann was up to. Using a stick smeared with lard, she coaxed Halfwolf out of his bed until he came to the end of his rope. Then she dashed in quickly, seized my blanket, and made off with it towards Ard Bruill's hut. She's sorry now for what she did to me, I thought.

Meanwhile, round the fire, Corag Mor left the circle and went off alone. The cups were filled again, the fire sizzled, and Breasal completed the joke by saying, 'Huh! You'll not be laughing when you've to make your own broth in future – mark my words!'

When I think what happened two nights later, I am tempted to believe that Corag Mor was right. The blue flame may indeed have been a warning in the fire.

CHAPTER 3

'There's your blanket,' she said, tossing the thing at my feet. 'I'm going down to the Round of Stones to see Oscar. Are you coming?'

I was sorry to see that blanket again. I was sorry to hear it mentioned again and I was ashamed to look at the lip I'd given her.

'Are you sure you want me along?'

'Yes. It's more fun when there's three.'

As we left the village by the goat path, Frann made a point of stopping in the copse where we stool willows.

'We're going to pretend something, Dinn Keene. We're going to pretend that I didn't give Halfwolf your precious sucking blanket and that you didn't wallop me on the mouth nearly knocking all my teeth out. Do you agree?'

Of course I agreed. The power of her standing there so windblown and beautiful and still would have terrified even her, had she known that she possessed it.

'All right. What are you and Oscar doing at the Round of Stones?'

'It's getting dark and there's magic there. Oscar says the stones used to be real people before a magician put a curse on them. Come on.'

Huh. And what does Oscar know, thought Dinn Keene.

A fitful little wind stirred the ribbons on the mountain ash as we climbed down to the stones.

Sly Oscar had prepared a dare for us when we arrived. 'You will walk the stones against the sun! And you must walk on top of them without falling off – or I'm the winner!'

I said at once that I wouldn't do it. Before I had finished speaking, Frann was up on the first stone, and already jumping to the second. I had no clear idea what evil she might bring down upon herself by this madness. I knew only that these stones were the mark of something larger than my understanding. Indeed, standing there in the wolf-light, I was prepared to grant that these 'stones' might well be the remains of people somehow changed by the dark arts of a magician, and that Frann was skipping from one immortal shoulder to the next. And just to claim a dare?

Then I heard the voices. I heard them plainly. And the look on Oscar's face told me that I had not made them up in my head, for he had heard them too.

I ran into the Round, seized Frann by the ankle, and hauled her to the ground on top of me.

'Cheating, Dinn Keene! You're trying to stop me winning the dare and you almost broke my neck!'

My fearful arms held her fast. 'It's the stones. Oscar heard them too.'

'What about them?'

'They're talking.'

She wriggled loose from me and swept the hair from her face. 'Talking stones? Are you trying to protect me from talking stones? Stupid old Dinn Keene, you're going red!'

I do not believe that I was going red, or that there was light enough for her to see me, even if I was. Suddenly Frann looked up, and stiffened. The silhouette of a person passed high above us, skirting the hollow. Breathlessly we pressed our backs against a stone, and waited.

Eight of them passed by, following in the first one's steps. Each one carried a long stick with twigs tied to the end, like a broom.

'Lake-dwellers,' Oscar whispered in my ear. 'That's Ogue Wormbeard out in front, leading them.'

Ogue of the Lake. His people lived on a man-built island near the shore – they were rarely seen. Sometimes he came to leave totems at the Round of Stone, but this time he had passed right by. So where was he going?

Frann said, in her normal voice, 'Perhaps they're going to do some trade with Ruadh.'

'What have they got to trade with?' said Oscar scornfully.

'Honey. And they make nice clothes out of fibres, Oscar. Or maybe they're just hunting.'

'In the dark?'

'*Badgers*, then. Come on, we'd better get back or they'll slay us.'

All the way home I had the feeling that something was going to happen. It was not a strong feeling – just the kind of skin-shiver we all get from time to time. Certainly it did not prepare me for what met my eyes. I looked and saw, and for a while I do believe that I felt nothing at all.

Ruadh's people lived in four south-facing huts at the foot of a hill. Each of the huts had long, sloping roofs of thatch which reached almost to the ground. One of these roofs was now alight.

Until this moment I, Dinn Keene, had always thought of fire as a slow, reluctant thing that needed patience: even as I watched, Chief Ruadh's hut was changed into a blazing round of crackling, leaping flame. Ogue of the Lake stood by, calmly watching his work. I heard the mad-dog bellowing of Ard Bruill, who thrashed so much that three men pinned him to the ground. Murta bravely tried to crawl from his hut, but was clubbed senseless and lay with his body blocking the door. I could not tell whether the cries of terror came from animals or people – perhaps it was simply my own voice that I heard.

'That'll do,' cried Ogue. 'Come away, Dara – be satisfied!'

His men passed right by me, for I was too stupid to hide, on their way to their boats and their fortress on the lake.

Such a fire, such a monster, could not be fought. It writhed and roared and spat into the night sky. Yet how we tried to put it out! Ard Bruill, Murta, Corag Mor, Bodman Tar, Eithne of the marrow bones and Breasal who was old, and young Ennis and his wife, and Laigan the cripple – even I, Dinn Keene, beat the fringes of the fire with branches until the inner poles gave way. And the roof collapsed, blinding us all with a final eruption of sparks and ash and heat.

After a while we sat down.

'Who is missing?' Ennis whispered.

Ard Bruill glanced at Oscar, whom Breasal had buried into her chest. He was Ruadh's natural son.

'All of them but him. Father, mother, daughters.'

'And the dogs,' I heard Frann breathe.

'Aye, and the two dogs.' Ard Bruill rose to cut free Halfwolf so that the poor creature could run and rid himself of his fear.

'I don't understand it,' said Bodman Tar, as he beat his great fist on his knee. 'They only burned one hut. Why? Why Ruadh? Why not all of us? Why any of us? What did we do to them? What?'

And he looked about him wild-eyed, knowing full well that not one of us could answer him – except for Corag Mor, who knew, but did not speak.

Dinn Keene felt the closeness as they waited, and the fire died down. His fostering-father was dead. One powerful emotion united them all.

Dinn Keene looked into the face of Ard Bruill, who now had the power that used to be Ruadh's. Ard Bruill said, 'Ogue will pay the full price.'

There was another feeling. It touched one, touched them all, Dinn Keene felt it too. After the sorrow, the anger was coming.

PART TWO

THE ROUND OF WOOD

CHAPTER 4

We began to build again.

We gave our huts stone walls and passages under the ground. This time we chose an open site where the slope ran down to the rushes at the water margins. And when the huts were finished we stripped whole young pines of their branches and stuck them in the earth so that they formed a great Round of Wood to shield us from our enemies. Around everything we created a ditch, digging deep to pile high. This ditch was closed by a stout gate, made by Murta.

The Lake-dwellers watched all our labours from their boats, a long way from shore. I, Dinn Keene, was put in charge of a section of the ditch, and I gave my commands to other children in a voice that grew deeper. Also, my body became stronger during that summer of heavy work, and I used to play the man of iron in front of Frann or else wheedle sympathy for my blisters. Sometimes she said to me, 'Don't be such a show-off, Dinn Keene,' and then I felt sour.

It was about this time that we met the Man of Speech.

Somewhere behind us, in the interior of the blue-stone hills, the stream began.

It was a running tumble of water which suddenly emerged from the barren rocks of Bad Pig's Gap into a lovely little glen. This was one of the favourite places of Frann, Oscar and Dinn Keene. They came here often, for just at the head of the glen the river jumped gloriously into a rock pool far below.

On this particular day when the wind was mild and the sun shone directly down through the split in the trees, those three friends stood under the spill of the water until they were thoroughly drenched. Then they climbed the rocks and stretched out on a warm slab to dry.

From here, one could see the river dropping through the glen in stages. After a dry period, the rocky banks looked like huge stepping stones laid out for a giant. Oscar saw the figure first.

He sat up on all-fours and stiffened like a deer. 'I see somebody coming!'

He stuttered as he spoke, and his eyes shimmered with fear. Frann took his hand, but that was not enough comfort for Oscar, who stood up and ran away.

'It *is* a person,' said Frann, peering. 'Come on, let's get out of here.'

Dinn Keene reached for his spear.

'It's one of the Lake-dwellers, Dinn Keene, will you come *on*.'

'I'm staying.'

'What for?'

'I'm going to fight him.'

'Don't be so stupid, Dinn Keene, he'll hit you one crack and open you up like an egg.' She slid off the rocks. 'I'm going for the others.'

'Get them, I don't care.'

Keeping low, Dinn Keene skipped up the stones at the side of the waterfall and lay down flat with a clear view downstream. It was strange, he thought, to see a Lake-dweller on his own now that the feud had started. Maybe he was after one of the goats.

Frann lay down beside him. 'All right, Dinn Keene, I'll stay with you. Just to make sure you don't do anything stupid.'

As the figure came closer, they saw that he was an oddity from head to toe. In his hand he carried a rough, unseasoned pole of shoulder height. He walked on bare feet, with his open-toed sandals round his neck. His tunic, finely woven, barely covered the knees and hardly seemed decent. His thick, dark hair had been cropped short – the scalp showed white above the ears where it had been sheared. Even Murta, thought Dinn Keene, Murta who was bald on top let his hair grow to hide his ears. This fellow had come to Grey Man Mountain from a long way off.

'Look at him! Where's he from?' whispered Frann.

The stranger stepped into the rock pool and turned his face upwards into the rushing water. Raising his hands, he began to sound out such a torrent of meaningless words that Dinn Keene gave a start, and was seen!

I, Dinn Keene, rose with my spear levelled, and I can say that the stranger did not flinch.

'My name is Ancell of Lyons and Tours,' he said, smiling. 'I guessed I wasn't alone – back there I saw goats with their horns trimmed. You are the first people I have seen since I beached my boat. Please come down.'

Meanwhile, Frann had poked her head over the waterfall. 'Where did you say? Are you trading something? What's in your pouch?'

'Come down and I'll show you. As a matter of fact, you can have some.'

Frann, always more free with her conversation and her trust than I, bounced down the rocks and waited while the stranger emptied his pouch.

'There. My friends on the island gave me honey in this little jar.'

'Do you mean the island on the lake?' I asked.

'I mean an island in the sea west of here. My friends, I have crossed mountains where the snow never melts, just to be here. But look what else I've got! There are no better oysters in the great towns of Gaul.'

He slit one with a metal blade, put it to his mouth, and emptied it. 'I picked them in the estuary. Of course they're two days old now, but still good. Have one.'

'Oh no, they're slimy,' said Frann. 'But can I

have the hard bit? It's beautiful.'

'The shell. Of course you can have it.'

'Don't take it from him!' I called out.

Coming down the rocks, I handled my spear confidently so that he would know I could use it if I had to. Apart from that knife, I didn't think he had a weapon.

'How did you get here?'

'In a horse-skin boat. Then I walked.'

'I know about people like you.'

'Do you,' said the stranger calmly. He seemed almost amused.

'You're one of the Wanderers who speaks strange words. Corag Mor told me about people like you. You're all mad.'

'I am not mad.'

'You stand in the water and shout at the sky.'

Ancell sat down and began to dry his feet. 'Listen, boy, I saw the blue sky through the trees, I felt the pure water on my face, I thought to myself: Look how the river enjoys itself! And I sang out my thanks for the beauty all around me. If that is madness – well then, yes, I am mad. What is your name?'

I did not give it.

'His name is Dinn Keene,' said Frann. 'He was

fostered on us years ago but his people have probably forgotten all about him. What is that round your neck?'

'It's a cross.'

'It's quite pretty,' said Frann.

'Yes, there are many stories to be told about this thing,' replied the stranger, turning to me. 'Dinn Keene – would you do something for me? Would you take me to your village?'

'We don't have a village, we only have five huts. You can find other places more important.'

'Everybody is important, Dinn Keene, whether they live in a palace or a cave. Help me up, please.'

I could see no reason why he could not get up by himself. It seemed obvious that he was using the moment to clasp hands and begin a friendship, so I wheeled away from him and took the path over the moor. The stranger and Frann followed behind, chatting easily. I felt cheated of her company.

Presently the stranger called out for me to stop. His interest had been caught by a mound of fresh sods.

'I've seen this sort of thing before. It's a grave, isn't it?'

I nodded. 'Yes.'

'Whose?'

'Ruadh. He was my fostering-father.'

'I see.'

'You don't see,' I replied. This stranger had never met Chief Ruadh and could not know the full value of him. 'That grave is lined with stones. Do you know how many days it took us to shift the biggest stone up here?'

'I don't know, Dinn Keene.'

'Well it was taller than you are. Tell him, Frann.'

But Frann was fiddling with her new toy, the oyster shell. 'I don't know either, Dinn Keene.'

'You would know if you had been pulling it!' I cried, thrusting out four fingers. 'There! Do you know anybody as important as that?'

Ancell the Wanderer approached the mound and stared at it thoughtfully. 'This makes me wish I had known your father. But all men and women are important.'

'He was not my father, he was my fostering-father. Ogue of the Lake killed him and soon it will be his turn to die.'

'And where is your fostering-father now, Dinn Keene?'

Such a question! Perhaps he is a madman after

all, I thought. 'What do you mean, where is he now?'

'Well, surely you believe that he was – and is – more than his flesh. What's in there ...' Ancell waved an airy hand at the sealed tomb '... there's more to a person than what's in there.'

'Do you understand magic?' asked Frann. 'I think you do. You *talk* as if you do!'

'I understand what happens when people die.'

'So does Corag Mor,' I said.

'And who is he?'

'Our priest. Come on.'

Now there came on the wind the beloved smell of peat smoke. The gleam of the lake rose into view, we saw the Round of Wood set back from the shore and the thatch of our huts within. As our pace quickened, Frann picked up some brittle wood and put the pieces in the stranger's hands.

'Carry these.'

'Twigs?' He laughed. 'But why?'

'We always bring back sticks when we've been away for a while. It's good luck.'

Word of our coming had gone ahead of us – Oscar's doing, no doubt. Those feet of Ancell's, which had walked the streets of Rome and distant towns, now took him through Murta's gate into the Round of Wood. I am not certain whether the Man of Speech deserves the credit or the blame, but I do know that our lives were about to change.

What an entrance Dinn Keene made that day! Everybody was looking at him, or rather, at the Man of Speech following behind like a wonderful prize. Eithne carried her baby out to see, all snuggly warm in the green sucking blanket.

Halfwolf, spinning in circles, almost strangled himself with the effort of trying to break away and eat the stranger, who stopped in front of Ard Bruill.

Ard Bruill wore the axe he'd taken from the ruins of the fire. Unlike Ruadh, he was a tall man, with the largeness some people like to see in a leader. To his astonishment, the stranger suddenly handed him a fistful of dirty old twigs, at which Bodman Tar sniggered loudly.

'Who is he?' Ard Bruill barked at Dinn Keene.

'I found him by the waterfall, he wanted to come here.'

'I have come a long way,' said the stranger. 'My name is Ancell of Lyons and Tours, God be praised that I have found you. It is written that all people shall hear the Truth, should they live at the very edges of the world, and it is for me to bring it to this place as my brothers have carried it into the land of the Friesian, the Saxon, the Lombard and the Frank.'

Ard Bruill raised the hairy caterpillars above his eyes. They met over his nose in confusion.

'Wait there a minute,' he said, retreating to cuff Halfwolf round the head until he fell quiet. 'Now. Where are you from?'

'Not from this land. I am from many different places. I came across mountains where the snow never melts to be here. I bring you words from the mouth of God.'

Ard Bruill sniffed. 'We don't get much snow around here,' he said, and glanced at the still face of Corag Mor as if to wonder what they were going to do with this oddity. Then he appeared to think of his stomach.

'Have you eaten? Eithne will give you food. Afterwards … Well, I don't know. I suppose you may come into my hut. We don't get many visitors here, you know.'

The meeting broke up into little groups, all buzzing with conversation. Corag Mor's eyes were set deep in his paint-stained face, and impossible to fathom. Yet I am certain that his heart was already set against the Man of Speech called Ancell.

That night, just before Murta closed the gate, Dinn Keene asked Frann to walk as far as the lake shore with him. Oscar wanted to come too, but Dinn Keene shook a fist at him behind Frann's back, and drove him away.

The sough of the wind in the rushes was a mournful sound to me that night – a note of great longing. I remember well that it matched my mood. It sounded like my own voice which had somehow become external to me. I did not understand the changes that were happening inside my head.

'He must have seen some wonderful things, that funny person,' she said. 'How do you like my shell, Dinn Keene?'

Already she had a string round the shell and wore it as an ornament just above the swell of her breasts.

'It's all right,' I said, looking away.

'Nobody else has one, Dinn Keene. You don't

know something special when you see it, that's the trouble with you.'

'I like it, it's nice! Maybe I like you the way you are. Anyway, I want to ask you something.'

Now she took to plaiting rushes. 'What do you want to ask me, Dinn Keene?'

'About today. When we were talking to the stranger you said that my people have forgotten about me.'

'And?'

'Well, *have* they? Do you really think that?'

'How would I know? I only said that because you were trying to puff yourself up like something important.'

'I am important!'

She laughed, and fitted the braid of rushes round my skull. 'One day they'll come and take you away and make you into a great chief.'

She had come close to me in order to fit me with my crown of rushes, and so I found my arms around her, pulling her tight. For a moment that I would have preserved for ever in amber resin if I could, she pressed herself along the length of me – then tapped me gently with one hand.

'Murta will be closing the gate. We have to go now.'

'If they do send for me … will you come away with me, too?'

I had asked as lightly as I could. She kept me waiting through the screeching of some wildfowl over the lake.

'I don't think so. I don't think I could do that, Dinn Keene.'

CHAPTER 5

I must introduce some new voices into my story (said old Dinn Keene).

You will understand that a blood-feud had begun between the Lake-dwellers on the one side, and my people in the Round of Wood on the other. I have given the impression that Ogue of the Lake was an evil being with the dark heart of a beast, and that my people were blameless. You shall judge, Patrick of the Pens, I no longer care so much. These things were long ago.

Let me say what was happening among the Lake-dwellers at this time, as it was afterwards told to Eithne as she nursed Ogue's wife, Falnamuir. She was a handsome woman, with slow-glancing eyes.

When evening came and the wolf-light left the

water, Ogue told his folk to hang the sacred parts of a young animal on the wattle fence of their man-made island. This would pacify anything that might walk in the night. He stood at the gate of the crannog, gazing over the narrow water to the bank. Once there had been a sturdy bridge here, but it had to come down when the feud began and they now went everywhere by boat.

Falnamuir joined him at the gate. 'You must go and see Ard Bruill,' she said. 'How long can we go on living like this? For three months we've hardly set foot on the land. That bank over there might as well be a far country.'

This was only the truth – they avoided the near shore for fear of ambush.

'Dara went out two nights ago,' said Ogue.

'And for what? A couple of woodcock and small game! It's a shameful way to hunt, and you know it.'

'We have fish.'

'We're sick of fish, Ogue. But being sick of fish is not the worst thing. The worst thing of all is the fear we live in. Go to Ard Bruill, he's a reasonable man. Tell him what happened. Let him know how Ruadh came across your daughter while she was gathering in the yew glen, undefended, and alone, and how he abused her. Take her with you, let them feel the child she's carrying! Offer him payment.'

On that word Ogue began to shake his head. 'He will ask for a blood-price.'

'Not if you explain. He will argue, you will offer more. It's better than creeping ashore like thieves – cowards by day and by night.'

'It's possible. Ard Bruill might listen.'

'Of course he'll listen. He has a daughter of his own, hasn't he? Think what that brute did to our Leah.'

'Corag Mor will not listen,' said Ogue. 'He is the one.'

And now Ogue stooped to lift the last of the boats from the water. There were several fish in it, still caught in the nets – whereupon Falnamuir, finding herself ignored, jumped into a boat and took up a paddle.

'Where are you going?'

'About as far as you could throw a stone,' she cried. 'Over there, into that forbidden land! I'm going to see our bees – the children cry out for something to sweeten their stir.'

The man called Emman was standing by and made a move to stop her, but Ogue checked him. 'No, let her go, let her see the hives.'

'But …'

'I want her to see the hives. You go with her.'

A few strokes carried Falnamuir into the roots of the Thunder-oak on the bank, where a night wind from the wood met her like a cold breath. Emman, who knew what danger they were in, led her to the coppice where the Lake-dwellers kept their bees.

It was a place of phantoms. Brave as she was, Falnamuir almost fled from there in terror. They were surrounded by pale shapes. Someone had skinned the bark off the trees for as high as a hand could reach. While her heart steadied, Falnamuir told herself that the fear was only in her mind.

But there could be no doubt that the place was cursed. In the bole of an old tree there sat a skull-sized stone, painted.

'How did it get here?' whispered Falnamuir.

'We think Corag Mor left it. There are other stones, all smeared with the juice of yew berries.'

'But why?'

'We must hurry,' said Emman. 'Look at the hives if you must – but hurry.'

The hives had not been damaged, but they were empty.

'Now you know,' said Emman. 'The place is

64

cursed. We have no bees. Come away.'

She found herself walking backwards from the naked trees. It's as if I'm being driven from the forest, thought Falnamuir, expelled by it. Could such a feeling be real?

They were met by Ogue, who pulled the boat dry.

'Well, now you know why the children go without honey. Corag Mor has left his totems all round the shore of the lake, we can't land a boat without seeing one. He means to damn us with magic.'

'But can he do that?'

'He has powers that go deep – always had, even before he went down to the plains. Even the bees do what they're told! Did you see the stone?'

Falnamuir rubbed at her forearms, which had come into pimples with the chill of the night air. She wanted to say that a stone was just a stone, but in her heart she could not believe it.

People (said old Dinn Keene) do not fear strangers when they come without weapons and alone. They will open their arms and their larders to the oddest kind of wanderer while they bicker without mercy with their family and their friends.

I say to you, Patrick of the Pens, that the most hospitable people may be those who will cheerfully murder their neighbours over a cow, a woman or a ditch. So it was with our Wanderer, the Man of Speech.

Ancell was no threat to us, so we made him welcome. He made himself a little tent from borrowed hides and became a familiar figure in the Round of Wood.

People appeared to like him. He told stories of great battles in the desert and the splitting of the sea; of holy men who walked in flames; of a boy who felled a giant with a stone; of ships as tall as the Thunder-oak; of a man who lived in the belly of a monstrous fish. It is no wonder that we named him the Man of Speech. He preferred to stay in the Round of Wood, talking to the women and children, rather than hunt a wild pig. We heard of a man-god who made blind eyes see and who fed a mountainside of people out of a basket of bread. Yes, we all listened to these stories of the God-all-Father and Mary's Great Son.

Almost all. One person did not listen. Corag Mor pretended to ignore Ancell, but I don't think any of us were fooled. Many a time I saw them looking at one another, each one bursting with curiosity about the other. And then one evening, I, Dinn Keene, learned that Corag Mor was afraid of the Man of Speech.

We had just eaten under an open sky on the flesh of young hares. Even Halfwolf lay on his belly with a bone between his paws. It was the lazy time of day, and Ard Bruill called for a jar of hazel-mead to be broken open, saying, 'The times are hard when a man has to fetch himself something to drink!'

'It's because you're so fussy!' snapped Breasal. 'There's good clear water at your elbow.'

'Don't talk to me about water,' said Bruill. 'If we were meant to drink water all the time we'd all have been fish. You'd have been a fine big trout in your day, Breasal.'

'Trout yourself,' muttered Breasal, settling herself by the fire. They might want her to sing, later.

'This is a waste,' grumbled Ennis. 'The wine is too young.'

'Get it down you! Wasn't it made from the honey of Wormbeard's bees? It'll be the most perfect stuff you ever tasted.' And Bruill raised his voice to shout, 'You, Wanderer – come over here, I want you.'

Ancell, who was with Murta, left his work and came over.

'Dip your tongue in this mead and give us an opinion. Is it on the young side, or what?'

So Ancell tasted the wine, and smacked his tongue round his mouth.

'Well?'

'Too sweet,' said Ancell. 'But … fair. It will improve.'

'Not this jar,' said Bruill, grinning. 'This one has no chance of improving. Tell me this, Wanderer, how does our food compare with all these wonderful places you've seen on your travels? The truth, now.'

'The truth is that you eat well. You have been well provided for.'

'By whom?' said Corag Mor. These were the first words Dinn Keene had heard him say directly to the stranger, and they caused a certain quietness. 'Provided by whom? Do you mean that our food has been provided by this great all-spirit you've been filling our heads with?'

Ancell did not answer for a moment. Then he

simply said, 'Yes.'

'Then where is this spirit now? Tell me a place where it can be found.'

'Within me.'

Ard Bruill smiled a great smile. Was it the young wine working already, Dinn Keene wondered, or that answer?

'Whereabouts inside you? What part?' he asked.

'In my thoughts. The Great One I speak of comes into the minds of people and causes Himself to swell.'

'He sounds a bit like barley in soup,' said Ard Bruill.

Even Ancell smiled. 'A little. All the same, this can happen to anyone who allows it to happen.'

'But what does all this mean?' said Corag Mor, shifting forward. 'You take into yourself a kind of power, then?'

'Yes, in a way. A kind of power.'

'Friend,' said Ard Bruill, tapping Ancell on the knee. 'Look what happened to the Thunder-oak when the bolt hit him. He shrivelled up. How can you take that kind of power into yourself, and stay the same?'

'It is a power that affects *people*,' Ancell replied evenly. 'And when *this* lightning strikes, the kind

I'm talking about, no other spirits will do for you, no matter how many of them you may think you have. They will seem weak and feeble beside the God-all-Father who has come into you, and grown large.'

By now we had all gathered round the Man of Speech, except for Oscar, who sat apart rolling worms of clay between the flats of his hands.

'This living God made the earth and the sun and the stars. He made the forest and the mountain and the rivers that run down to the sea. His perfect finger draws the rainbow. He is the cause of everything that lives and grows, whether it is a tree or one of your children. And yes,' – here Ancell paused to look at Corag Mor – 'He is the provider of your food.'

In the silence, Ard Bruill bent his elbow for a swallow. 'Well, he sounds useful, this … whatever. How do you know all this stuff?'

'There are books.'

'What's that?'

'It doesn't matter. I know because I talk to Him.'

'Talk? You just … talk? How?'

Ancell seemed to be as amused as Bruill. 'I can easily show you,' he said.

In a moment he had lowered himself to his

knees in front of Bruill, who beamed down at him, delighted at the way things were turning out.

'Wait! Frann – go waken Bodman Tar, he won't want to miss this! Talk out loud, Wanderer, so that we can all hear. And don't use those funny words they have across the sea. Which one are you going to talk to, the God-all-Father or Mary's Great Son? Do you want quiet?'

'Quiet is best.'

'I thought so!' And Bruill bellowed out for a hush to fall on the Round of Wood.

Corag Mor swept to his feet. 'I'm against this,' he said.

'Why?' inquired Bruill huffily.

'Because we don't know what this fool is going to say! Haven't we spirits of our own that we know and are sure of? And we know that they are quick to feel anger. Let him not speak in the Round of Wood for the sake of a drunken game.'

Now Corag Mor's influence over this company was great, and Ard Bruill could not ignore it. Yet he would not give up his entertainment. Indeed, perhaps the challenge to his authority spurred him on.

'Go outside!' he said, pointing to Ancell. 'Do your talking on the lake shore and we can watch you from here. That way you can please me and satisfy Corag Mor. Come on!'

The Man of Speech did not try to hide his amusement at all this. After leaving the Round of Wood with a smile on his lips, he fell to his knees near the lake and turned his face upwards. Bruill and those who were tall enough peered over the fence; others watched from the gate. Dinn Keene had never seen so many people made so curious by the same thing.

'I wonder what he's saying?' Bruill muttered aloud. 'That is a peculiar individual, Corag Mor.'

'The man's a fool.'

'Then it can do no harm to listen to his stories.'

'Ard Bruill, the man is a fool, but a dangerous one. I think he has Murta half-convinced about this person called Mary's Great Son. And as for Eithne, she believes every word he says. Send him away.'

Ard Bruill gave a sly chuckle. 'Suppose he's right and there is a Great One? Why would he come all this way to tell us lies?'

'His thoughts have the simplicity of madness. You can't just decide to get down and have a little chat with those we can't see and can never fully understand. To come into the presence of what

72

he calls a god is to wait, is to fast, is to listen, to tremble – do you seriously believe that the Otherworld makes silly word-bargains with us? No! They demand that we give them something. Life. Corn. Totems. To bring your mind close to a spirit is to … to touch the lightning. It is an awesome thing and that man is a fool. Send him away.'

'We'll see,' said Bruill. 'Here he comes. Well, Wanderer, what did you say to your … whatever?'

'Several things. I asked Him whether I should stay here or go further.'

'And did he talk back to you?'

'He said I am to stay here – if Ard Bruill agrees, of course.'

'What do I know about these things!' shouted Bruill, glancing at Corag Mor. 'Stay or go, go or stay – what does it matter to me?'

Our chief hurried away to attack the remains of his mead; Corag Mor stayed a moment longer to challenge the Man of Speech with paint-darkened eyes.

I, Dinn Keene, knew that some kind of combat had already been joined.

CHAPTER 6

Frann, Oscar and Dinn Keene were on the lake shore in the early morning. Oscar and I had slings with us, Frann had Eithne's baby in her arms. From time to time she cuddled the baby and told him that he was so lovely she could just eat him.

'I saw you the other night,' Oscar whispered to me.

'What do you mean, you saw me?'

'Trying to kiss her. I was watching and it didn't work because she didn't let you kiss her.'

I almost spat at Oscar, that spoiler of my happiness. 'I wasn't trying to kiss her! And mind your own stinking business instead of spying on me, you lump of bird-dirt!'

This didn't bother him. It made him worse.

'Anyway, she let me kiss her.'

'You're a liar.'

'I'm not a liar, it was in the Round of Stones. On the mouth. She closed her eyes.'

'I'm going to ask her.'

'She won't want to talk about it,' said Oscar.

Dinn Keene flew as straight as a crow to where Frann jogged the baby on her knees.

'What are you looking at me like that for, Dinn Keene?'

'Because Oscar told me something!'

'And so?'

'He says … that you like him better than me.'

'And I'm to blame for everything Oscar says, am I?'

'Well, do you?'

Up she rose with the baby in her arms. 'Look, you and Oscar can argue all you like for as long as you like. You always have. Just leave me out of your stupid talk.' And she walked to the edge of the water just as a wedge of wild geese came flying in to land.

I slipped a stone into my sling and stepped into the water determined to hit either a goose or an Oscar – I wasn't fussy which.

'Don't you dare, Dinn Keene,' Frann said

crossly. 'You'll get us into trouble if you hit one of those birds.'

She meant that the spirits of dead people were known to use such birds to make long journeys. Perhaps at this moment, I thought, the immortal part of Ruadh is on the water, wrapped up in one of those geese. They sailed over sunken clouds, ever closer as if to taunt the sling and me. Suddenly their wings began to whirr. They ran on the water as if they had guessed what was in my mind.

Then we saw what had really startled them.

A boat was coming – one of those light canoes used by the Lake-dwellers. The two men inside struck slowly, and in time. I could not believe that they intended to bring their boat ashore at this particular point; and yet they didn't stop.

By now Oscar bristled like a wild beast. I told him to run and warn Ard Bruill in case this was an attack.

'They couldn't be attacking us,' said Frann, 'there's only one boat.'

'What do they want, then?'

'I don't know, Dinn Keene – hold the child and I'll swim out and ask them!'

I still had the sling in my hand, tempting me.

Lake-dwellers were not protected by rules as the wild geese were. They glanced over, saw me and my sling, and took no notice. Their boat scraped on the shallow bottom of the margins as they pulled it half-dry.

The mystery now grew cloudier still, for the Lake-dwellers, standing on our shore, took a length of thin twine and used it to bind the left arm of one to the right arm of the other; and in this way, lashed together, they began to walk towards the Round of Wood. Frann and I followed as far as the entrance.

Here, Bodman Tar met them. Also, Murta and Halfwolf, who shook with rage as if he remembered the smell of those two from that awful night. The dog's muzzle had been removed so that the Lake-dwellers had to make themselves heard above the din coming from that mouth.

'We have tied our arms to show that we come in peace.'

Bodman Tar smiled. Perhaps that is not quite the word, for the movement of his lips left his face as sour as I have ever seen it. But he stepped aside.

As the heels of our visitors rattled on Murta's bridge, I confess that they seemed like brave men to me. How could they expect to leave the Round of Wood alive?

Then Ard Bruill appeared with the metal axe shining on his belt. His hair was wet and flat to his head after bathing. One of the visitors was too frightened to look at him directly, but the other spoke up. His name was Dara.

'Ogue wants to make an agreement. He hopes we can return to the understanding we used to have.'

Bruill spoke first to Murta. 'Shut that thing up before it deafens us. Now speak up,' he said, turning, 'what kind of agreement?'

'He wants to offer you payment for … for the death of Ruadh. We will pay his full worth.'

There was cold merriment in Ard Bruill's eyes as he sat on a log and signalled to Frann. She began to work with his damp hair.

'His full worth, you say?'

'Yes, his full worth.'

'I take it that you'll also pay the full worth of his daughters, the mother of his daughters, and the animals who died with them? I can hear those hounds baying, still.'

To this day, Dinn Keene remembers the hot eyes of the man called Dara as he spoke.

'Ruadh was to blame! He started the trouble, no-one but him.'

Ard Bruill reached up and stopped Frann's hand. 'Explain yourself.'

'I was to have Ogue's daughter as a wife. Your fine chief came across her in the yew glen while she was gathering. Stooped over, no doubt. And he brutally abused her. You can think up the details for yourself.'

Ard Bruill swept Frann aside, and came to his feet with terrifying menace.

'Who says this?'

'The girl says it! Leah's belly is out to here with shame. You can come and inspect her if you like!'

By now they were both shimmering with rage, and aware of their audience. We were all there. Dara, steadied by his friend, continued quietly.

'But Ogue says that we went too far. We offer hides of badger and goats, enough to make clothes for four people. Also two large stones of salt. Ten curds. One leather-hide boat filled with fuel from our turf piles, and you may keep the boat in which it comes. Ogue says you may ask for other things I haven't mentioned since you may have particular needs. And as a token of faith he will send you corn-ale and you may keep the vessel in which it comes.'

Dara glanced at his friend. This one, called Emman, nodded timidly, as if afraid that his head would roll off his shoulders. 'That is all.'

So tight a silence now occurred that Dinn Keene expected to hear it snap about his ears. Ard Bruill's eyes flitted about without lighting on any person before he spoke again.

'I hope Ruadh is listening, wherever he is. Now he knows what he's worth.'

'We have offered what we can,' said Dara. 'Will you accept our payment?'

'It's not just for me to say. Ruadh was a proud man, his spirit might be offended by your terms. On matters like these Corag Mor speaks for us all, and he was a full brother.'

The strange thing is, that of all the people present that morning, Corag Mor appeared to be the one who took least interest in the events now unfolding. Instead, he had quietly collected a small pile of stones between his feet. Dinn Keene noticed that he had found a vivid yellow stain for his face. This new colour along the sharp bones of his cheeks gave him the aspect of a predator.

Quietly, he said, 'We do not accept your price. You have not offered Ruadh's full worth.'

Dara looked to Ard Bruill, but found little comfort there. 'What is his full worth?'

'Ogue himself, and one other. It is a blood-price.'

The bound men glanced helplessly at one another. Dara straightened his gaze and shook his head defiantly. 'No.'

Corag Mor took up one of the stones at his feet. 'You will pay. By these stones, I curse Ogue and his line. Go back and tell him that his children shall drink whey-milk and grow feeble, in his camp he shall smell death. Go back, tell him he is cursed until these stones, these same stones, are gathered together in one place again.'

And, slowly turning against the sun, Corag Mor flung the stones away from him, one by one, in every direction.

Then he added, 'And remember to tell him also that a curse, once given, must fall.'

But a new force had come into the man called Dara – I, Dinn Keene, heard it in the powerful rasp of his voice. 'I will tell Ogue that he is cursed. As for you, Corag Mor, I have something to tell you, and it is this: yes, a curse once given, must fall. But a curse wrongly given returns and falls on the one who gave it. I mean you, Corag Mor.

You are the one who will smell death.'

Dara collapsed, screaming. With a swift downward lunge, as if paddling a boat, Corag Mor had driven the tip of his spear into the man's thigh. The other one, Emman, made a louder noise still, though he had not been touched. Corag Mor's arm rose again, perhaps to strike again, I do not know – for the man called Ancell ran forward and put himself between them. Then Dara, with the help of his friend, limped towards the gate.

No-one pursued them, or even watched them go. Something more compelling was happening. The spear of Corag Mor had come to rest, lightly, on Ancell's chest.

He'll strike, thought Dinn Keene. Truly, I was sure that the Man of Speech had but a few more breaths to take.

Ard Bruill spoke. 'Explain yourself, Wanderer, this is our business.'

'The God of my thoughts is the Father of us all. Killing within His family offends Him, I must say to you.'

'And our enemies?' barked Bruill. 'How are we to deal with our enemies?'

'We forgive them as best we can in the name of Mary's Great Son, who forgave us. It is the hardest thing in the world to do – but even if we can't, we can at least avoid this man's deliberate cruelty. We forgive!'

'And forget,' said Bruill, with bitter amusement. 'Well, it sometimes happens that they do not forgive *us*. Isn't it a pity that they come after us with spears and stones and torches in the night. Put away your weapon, Corag Mor, you were right. The Wanderer is a fool.'

The spear did not come down.

'I am not afraid of Corag Mor,' said the Man of Speech. 'I smile at the spear that shakes in his hand. Strike! Send me to the God-all-Father who will wash my hair and make me welcome.'

Corag Mor looked calm enough. Dinn Keene had seen him like this before, turned brittle, as water becomes ice. The spear did not come down until Ard Bruill took possession of it and tossed it away.

'Enough of this,' he said, returning to the log where Frann resumed her grooming.

PART THREE

THE ROUND OF WATER

CHAPTER 7

Not long after these events, Dinn Keene went looking for Ancell. There was a great plan building up inside my head for which I needed help. I found him talking with Eithne about the baby she would soon have, so I had to wait while the Man of Speech told how Mary's Son of Peace was born where they keep animals – and yet princes came to see him with gifts. I noticed that Eithne wore an emblem of crossed sticks round her neck.

At last Ancell had time for me. 'Well, Dinn Keene, where is your friend Frann? Don't tell me she has gone away and left you all alone?'

'She's gathering for Breasal.'

'Ah, good. Not with Oscar, I hope.'

'I want to show you something if you're not busy.'

'Is it far?'

'We have to leave the Round of Wood, but it's not far.'

Several times I looked behind me as I walked, expecting to find him breathless, but he had a light body and could easily match my brisk pace.

'Dinn Keene, wait – do you see over there? It's the tip of a tree.'

'Come on, that's not where we're going.'

'All the same, give me time to look.'

In this way the Man of Speech discovered the sacred hollow where our people asked favours from the Otherworld. A look of wonder came over his face as his eyes took in the ribbons on the rowan tree and the stones below.

'I should have known,' he said. 'Even here – even *here* – the pagans have their temple!' Then he hurried down, full of questions. 'Who made this place?'

'I don't know, it's been here since the beginning.'

'What beginning?'

'The first beginning,' said Dinn Keene, irritated. 'It's very old, that's all I know, probably older than Bad Pig's Gap.'

'But how do you use it?'

'Look, ask Corag Mor if you want to know.'

When Ancell suddenly took my arm, I felt the eagerness in his fingers. 'Do all your people believe in the power of these stones?'

'Yes.'

'Help me, Dinn Keene, bring me stones from over there, many stones.'

'What size?'

'All sizes. Come on!'

So I brought him stones, the only thing there was plenty of in those hills. And Ancell began to build. First he made a column as tall as my head. Then we raised a narrow slab to rest as a crosspiece on the column he had built. The work was easily finished with some smaller pieces to continue the upright pillar.

And now he knelt down to say some words in the secret language of the God-all-Father.

Before leaving we looked down from the rim of the hollow at the ancient round, the living ash, and the new thing we had made.

'Well, Dinn Keene? What do you think?'

'I don't think Corag Mor's going to like it.'

Which made him laugh out loud, though I hadn't been joking. 'Come on, you want to show me something. Is it far now?'

'Just over the next hill.'

'Then we'll *run!*'

We came upon the huts abruptly. Two of them had caved in and nettles grew already in the thatch. But the third hut had no roof to speak of – only two fallen beams, black all over and almost burned through where the fire had done its worst. Even the walls were scorched. What had once been Chief Ruadh's dwelling-place resembled the cold hearth of a giant.

I, Dinn Keene, remembered everything as I stood there: the thatch cracking louder than snapping whips; the howls of Halfwolf; shadows in the blazing light; and poor desolated Oscar urinating in old Breasal's lap.

'They made me look at my fostering-father in the morning, but I didn't know him.'

I felt Ancell press my shoulder, briefly. 'Tell me about Ruadh.'

'Tell what?'

'Was he a good man, for example?'

'What do you mean by "good"?'

'Worthy of being loved.'

'Yes, he was. The Lake-dwellers are lying about him the way they lie about everything. Ancell, I want you to teach me how to talk to the God-all-Father like you taught Eithne and Murta.'

'So that's why I'm here!' The Man of Speech smiled, yet examined me with looks. 'And so I will. But I have to warn you, Dinn Keene, that it takes patience and it takes time.'

I fell eagerly to my knees, which was the correct position from all I had seen. 'What do I do? Do I just start talking or are there magic words?'

'It's not simply a matter of talking. You have to listen, too.'

'*You* do it for me! Tell the God-all-Father he has to help me kill Ogue of the Lake like the boy who killed the giant with a stone.'

'Wait,' said Ancell carefully. 'Are you telling me that you intend to kill someone?'

'By fire. I have a good plan.'

'But, Dinn Keene, that is a dreadful ambition. You ... you are so young.'

'Old enough to die in that fire,' I said, 'if I had been there that night.'

'You don't understand. You are innocent of all the crimes and sins that time brings to all men. This is not the right thing to do.'

'Are you saying you won't help me?'

'I will help you to see clearly if you'll let me, yes!'

How he disappointed me, that Man of Speech!

He did not see Dinn Keene clearly enough, for all his peering. He did not see into the bitter part of me where I still hurt. He did not see that vengeance was far more than my right, it was also a duty that was calling me.

'Listen to me, Dinn Keene. You are not ready to talk to the God-all-Father. You will not be ready until you understand that all men are brothers of yours and that somehow, you have to work out a way of living in peace with them.'

'That's stupid!'

'No. That is what the Cross of Stones means. That is exactly what it demands of us, and nothing less.'

'I'll get him! I don't care if you help me or not, I'll still get him!'

'Dinn Keene, wait ...'

I heard no more. Away I went, so fast along our old paths that I soon lost him although he tried to follow me. My head was a simmering soup of rage and disappointment and remembered grief; the world was misty.

Yet I still had my plan! Kingfrog Ogue was not safe from me. I, Dinn Keene, would destroy him in his Round of Water, that Ducknest, with or without the magic of the Wanderer's great spirit.

CHAPTER 8

Late one evening, Frann, Oscar and Dinn Keene lay down on beds of dry rushes in the middle of the Round of Wood, near the fire. Tonight, we would sleep with nothing but clouds between us and the stars.

It was that time of evening when Murta closed the gate, and Halfwolf's tail began to wag because he knew that the muzzle would soon be off his mouth. In the little daylight left to us, Eithne cleaned the small game from Bascoign's snares, and the Man of Speech talked quietly to Laigan the cripple at the door of his makeshift tent. A satisfying darkness was falling over the Round of Wood.

Ard Bruill came over to the common fire, to save the ashes.

'What's this, then?' he said, seeing the three of us stretched out at his feet.

'We're sleeping outside tonight,' said Frann.

'What for?'

'Daddy, we were too warm in the hut last night, I couldn't get to sleep.'

'Huh.' Ard Bruill drummed his fingers on his belt suspiciously. 'Next week you'll be too cold! Sleep on the roof for all I care, wake up with dew on your faces – just don't come crawling into the hut during the night. And be sure you stay in the middle – you understand me, Frann?'

He smoothed a mixture of fine ash and powdered peat over the fire, and left us.

The moon that night was no bigger than a spat-out fingernail; and the clouds, driven on a soft wind of summer, held no threat of rain. The cry of Eithne's baby kept me awake for a long time. What would it be like, I wondered, if her second baby bawled as much as the first one. They would be a fine pair in the middle of the night.

Lying there, my body sometimes touched with Frann's. Of course, I arranged for this to happen by accident as often as possible. The excitement of one knee knocking on another, or even clashing elbows, was almost unbearable; and yet I fell asleep.

But I hadn't meant to sleep at all! And the moon, when I wakened, had shifted so much that I almost panicked. Was the night nearly over?'

'Frann!' I whispered, shaking her. 'Wake up, it's time!'

Oscar, too, opened his eyes. 'Get the bone,' I hissed at him.

There was even a bone in my plan in case Halfwolf should hear us. Meanwhile my head was turning light as I blew into the fire and blew again and again to redden the ashes. As they glowed, Frann scooped them into a clay pot with a narrow neck.

'That's enough, Dinn Keene, it'll be too hot to carry.'

'I'll put a cord round the neck. Fill it up!'

Oscar went over the gate first, then me with the clay pot, then Frann. My legs trembled with an intense, shut-in excitement as we stole away from the Round of Wood into the night – three shadows. The low path round the lake shore was shapeless in the dark, yet we travelled it with such familiarity that it might have been day. Many times I glanced over my shoulder at the hump of

Grey Man Mountain, and begged the sun not to rise.

There was, probably, a kind of madness driving us through the bracken and rushes of the margins that night; we scarcely slowed down even to blow into the ashes. But we were checked, finally, by the looming outline of Thunder-oak and the dwelling-place beyond.

It was a mere sling-shot away.

Nothing stirred in the Ducknest.

'Dinn Keene,' Oscar whispered, 'maybe ...'

'What?'

He wanted to go back, I could tell that his will to continue had drained away. As I spoke I wove twists of dry straw into my hair.

'Oscar, you stay here, some of them might have been night-hunting.'

'And what if they come?'

'Shout! You hear me? And then run. Frann, you come after me and bring the spear and keep it dry.'

'Nnn,' she replied – a peculiar little sound.

The Lake-dwellers, as well as removing their bridge, had cleared the bank down to short grass, so I crawled on my belly and slid into the water by holding on to the roots of Thunder-oak. While the water remained shallow – three steps, maybe four – I walked with my knees bent, keeping only my shoulders and the clay pot above the water. As the water deepened I straightened my legs. The island grew larger and still nothing stirred.

If the water was cold, I did not feel it. A short swim on my back, and my hand touched land! I remember well that my hand glowed with the thrill of it.

In a hurry now, I heaped the ashes against the base of the wattle fence, coaxing them into new life with soft breaths. By the time Frann arrived with the spear I was already feeding the small red glow with some of the straws from my hair. As the fence took light I stood to look into the crannog.

To my surprise Ogue's Ducknest seemed much like our own Round, though a little smaller, and so the huts were closer together. A turf pile I saw; stooks of willow reeds; a huddle of shapes which I took to be boats; and there were, besides, three milking goats tied to a post. These and other details should have warned me that behind me the sky was brightening.

Now I lit the spear, prepared for this moment with lashings of twigs and straw. Flame spurted up the shaft. There was no way of knowing which hut was Ogue's, so I let loose the spear at the largest roof. The tip bit into the thatch and stuck there, swaying. The tugging at my leg was Frann, urging me to come away – when I looked down at her in the water her eyes shone in the light from the burning fence.

But Dinn Keene had to wait some moments longer. I had to be sure that the blazing spear did its work. In excitement and terror I watched the flames feed joyfully on the roof, then a shout made me aware of the danger I was in, and I hurled myself towards the black water.

Was it Oscar who had shouted? Or Frann? It may have been one of the people from the stricken hut, I do not know. Even as I surfaced I knew that something was after me. A splash happened. Frann, striking for shore? Or a boat being launched? By now I was on my feet, driving my thighs through the clinging water. Something fell from nowhere and whipped the feet from under me. They dragged me backwards, away from Thunder-oak, more under the water than out of it.

Of course Dinn Keene fought the net that had claimed him, but it was a useless struggle. A fist dragged me to my feet. I was right at the centre, so it seemed, of a great rushing in my ears when I found myself looking straight into the face of Ogue of the Lake, Wormbeard himself; then my mind left me and went somewhere else.

I did not know, then, that they had captured Frann as well.

CHAPTER 9

When the sun came up over Grey Man, we were not missed in the Round of Wood.

There was no reason why we should have been missed before the common breakfast – most likely they thought we had wakened with a cold dew on our faces and made an early start on one of the duties we all had. The gate had been closed, cooking had begun, Halfwolf had been muzzled, before Bascoign noticed something strange on the lake shore.

'Bruill, come here and see this. Watch that elder bush near the water.'

'Who is it?'

'Young Oscar.'

Oscar ran into view, stood in the open for a

while, then darted behind the tree once more.

'Why is he howling like a stuck pig?' said Bruill, fascinated. 'I worry about that one, you know. He's getting worse instead of better.'

'I thought it was a game,' said Bascoign, 'but he's by himself.'

Bascoign sent his son out with the message that Oscar was to come at once for his breakfast. The boy came back bursting with news.

'He says he won't come but the Lake-dwellers have got Frann and Dinn Keene. Ogue Wormbeard got them in the middle of the night.'

The news, no doubt, sounded incredible. Yet the three rush beds still lay by the fire. Ard Bruill opened his mouth and sounded out Oscar's name.

When poor Oscar came into the Round of Wood, it was as if something was towing him against his will. He had suffered an hour's worth of torture on his own, convinced that he was in more danger from Bruill than from wild beasts.

'Speak!' Bruill barked at him.

'We ... we went over to their island.'

'What for?'

'To set them on fire,' cried Oscar.

'You went over to their island? To set them on *fire*?'

Others were arriving. Oscar looked at each of them in turn, to make them understand. 'It was Dinn Keene, he had the idea. We had ashes in a pot.'

'Ashes in a pot?'

'They were hot ashes.'

Ard Bruill dashed Oscar to the ground with a blow. 'Ashes in a pot? Are you stupid, you hog's head? I'll give you ashes! Do you think they are fools, like you? Have you any idea of the trouble you've put us in, you useless goat's toe? Ashes in a pot!'

Oscar had the wit not to answer these questions. All the grown people of the Round now gathered together in one place. For the purposes of the meeting, Ancell was included – or at least, no-one bothered to object. Ard Bruill flapped his arms at them.

'What are we going to do?'

'Surely we have to go and see them,' said Murta.

'Why?' asked Bodman Tar fiercely.

'Well at least we can explain that they weren't sent out by us. Say it was high spirits, youthful stupidity. Maybe we can talk through some kind of bargain. Get Frann back at least.'

Bascoign nodded, as if this made sense. Now

it was Corag Mor's turn to speak. 'I want to remind you that the boy Dinn Keene is important too. When his father comes he will expect to find a full-grown young warrior and it will go hard with us all if we can't give him one – you know that's true, Bruill.'

'It'll go hard with someone,' said Ard Bruill, 'if I lose my Frann. What do you say about this, Man of Speech?'

'Murta is right, I think. The first thing is to talk and find out what happened. It's even possible, after all, that our two young people are no longer alive.'

In the meantime Bodman Tar had returned to the company with a strung bow, which he thrust forward. 'There's the only kind of talk the Duck-people understand. They're on our backs, climbing all over us. I say we attack or they'll have us like whipped dogs.'

'You can talk, Bodman Tar,' said Eithne, 'they're not holding your son or daughter.'

Ard Bruill sat quietly for a moment, ruminating darkly. Then he took Laigan by the shoulder.

'Laigan, I want you to stay here in the Round in case they row in from the lake. Close the gate after we've gone. This one can stay, too.' He meant Ancell.

'That one should come with us,' sneered Bod-man Tar. 'He could talk the Lake-dwellers to death.'

They broke up to fetch their weapons.

Rohan, who was Bascoign's boy, beat out a slow rhythm on the skin of a leather-hide boat. The noise spread outwards from the moist air beneath the Thunder-oak to where it was aimed – the dwelling on the lake. In the still water a second crannog could be seen shimmering below. Ard Bruill tapped the boy on the arm.

'That'll do for now. They know we're here.'

'So where are they?' grunted Bodman Tar, letting go an arrow in sheer frustration. It thudded into one of the cone-shaped roofs on the island.

The afternoon, though still mild, had fetched in a drifting mizzle which made everything wet, and vague, and leaden-coloured. Not even the sky above could boast an independent cloud in the universal gloom.

Ennis said, 'They're inside, sitting at a warm fire. We're out here getting soaked.'

'You want us to go back, Ennis?' snarled Bodman Tar. 'A drip at the end of your nose and you quit?'

'That's enough,' said Bruill. 'How is talk like that going to help?'

After glaring at Ennis as if he was a worm worthy of stepping on, Bodman Tar swung himself into the lower branches of Thunder-oak, and began to climb.

Already – so it seemed to Bruill – they had been here a long time without a sight of anyone across the water. To be ignored, he did not mind so much; his worry went deeper than that. How was Frann? he wondered.

There was suddenly a clattering of noise in Thunder-oak.

'Arrows!' called Bodman Tar. 'They're letting fly at me. The Leechlegs are at home after all!' He dropped to the ground. 'They don't like me up their precious tree.'

Bruill looked into the tree, then across the lake, measuring the distance. One by one he considered the details: would it reach? Almost certainly. The top branches would smash the wattle hurdles, perhaps. And the trunk of the tree would make a bridge.

Could they cut it down? The metal axe was already in Bruill's hand as he turned to Corag Mor with a question. 'Answer me this – what would it cost us if we brought this tree down?'

'I would be against it.'

'Why? How would it affect us?'

'You know as well as I do that our kind may only take the dead wood, fruit and foliage from a life-tree. Nothing more.'

'The thing has already been half killed by lightning,' Ard Bruill pointed out.

'And still it stand there,' said Corag Mor. 'Who knows what makes use of it? It was there before any of us and I say let it be until it's ripe for the storm.'

But Ard Bruill could not wait for the storm. He began to strike. And after him, Murta took his turn with the axe.

'Wait!' cried Ennis. 'Look there.'

Something stirred within the lake-dwelling. At first it appeared that they were about to launch one of their canoes in the most awkward way possible – that is to say, *over* the wattle fence, without opening their hurdle-gate.

But when the boat came to rest upright on its point, the purpose of this activity became clear. Dinn Keene was lashed to the bottom of the boat. He hung there upside down.

'I saw him move,' said Corag Mor. 'At least he's alive.'

Now the hurdle-gate was taken away. As the man called Dara slipped into the water, Bodman Tar quietly fitted an arrow to his bow. From a point half-way to the bank, and waist-deep in water, Dara called out.

'You can see what's happening! If you cut down Thunder-oak the first thing it hits will be the boy. And tell the one with the bow to put it down. If I don't go back, your daughter's hair will be wet with her own blood!'

Ard Bruill knocked down the bow with his own hand. 'Give me back the girl.'

'We will return them both to you – we don't want this feud, it is doing us both harm. In good faith, why will you not accept our payment for the life of Ruadh?'

Murta broke the silence quietly. 'Take it, Bruill.'

'There is only one thing that we ask,' called Dara. 'That man there, Corag Mor, must lift his curse.'

Ard Bruill looked painfully at Corag Mor, for he knew that this one thing was not in his gift. Now Corag Mor came to the water's edge so that his feet were standing on the bare roots of the Thunder-oak, and his voice rang out so loudly that it was heard even by poor upside-down Dinn Keene.

'You saw the stones scattered, you were there, we all saw them. Stones cannot come together, words cannot be unsaid, the curse must fall!'

Dara remained long enough to cast a bitter look at the figure with the matted hair standing in the raindrops of Thunder-oak. He knew there could be no appeal.

'The boy will remain where he is until you leave,' he said to Ard Bruill, then returned to his island.

The company returned empty-handed to the Round of Wood, and avoided looking one another in the eye. Frann and Dinn Keene were still alive, but this felt like a defeat.

CHAPTER 10

We were treated well enough, I suppose. Life was never comfortable for us, but I cannot pretend that we were abused in any way. Sometimes they kept us indoors, sometimes they put us out. The worst thing, apart from the boredom of it all, was not knowing how long we would be there, for Ogue's Ducknest could not be stormed from the land or attacked from water without horrible risks.

There were as many grown-ups, I think, as we had in the Round of Wood. Ogue himself had a great eye for gutting fish – I have a clear memory of him slitting pike over a rush apron, and glancing at me with fun in his eyes, as Ruadh used to do.

'Wormbeard! That's not nice. What a name to

give a person. I think it's even worse than Leechlegs. What else do they call me over there?'

'Kingfrog,' I said.

Immediately Frann nipped me hard on the thigh to warn me that I might go too far with this name-calling. This was our third day of captivity and we were pinned to the ground by the same peg.

'Kingfrog! Now there's a name for a hero.'

Ogue turned merrily to the girl who sat on her own in the dimmest part of the hut. 'I hope you realise, Leah, that you're looking at a *king*.'

The girl did not reply, which did not surprise me. I hadn't heard her say a word in three days.

'Leave her be,' whispered Falnamuir, who was gutting the same batch of fish. 'Her thoughts are somewhere else.'

'How long are you going to keep us here?' I asked.

Ogue held up his apron, and the guts of many a fish slipped into a jar. 'Who knows? This is a bad feud, no telling how it will end. Corag Mor must lift his curse.' Then he brightened, and turned heartily to Frann. 'How much do you two like one another, eh? A little? Quite a lot? She doesn't answer! I think I'm doing you a favour, tying you up so close.'

Falnamuir gave Frann a sympathetic smile, then went out with Ogue and left us alone with the girl.

This girl, Leah, sniffled in a corner. We knew already that Falnamuir was worried to death about her, and with good reason. It seemed to me that she lived as a snail does, completely shut up in a house of her own.

Sitting there, tied up, Frann took my hand. Since we could not be rescued, we were hostages at Ogue's pleasure until an agreement could be reached, or until we escaped ourselves. This understanding, as well as the actual touching of our bodies, brought us closer together.

On the fourth day of our captivity the Duckpeople took Frann and me outside and tied us to a post. Through the afternoon there was much coming and going, especially by women. I made a face at two small children who had been throwing crumbs of peat at us.

'Don't you feel stupid sitting here?' I said to Frann. 'Doesn't it make you feel like a goat?

Maybe that's why they moved us, they want us to feel like goats.'

'Don't you really know why they moved us, Dinn Keene?'

'To make us think we're goats.'

She sighed impatiently. 'That girl, Leah, is having her baby.'

In that case, thought Dinn Keene, I'm glad they tied me to a goatpost.

A while later we heard the first cries of the youngest little Lake-dweller. It sounded surprisingly fierce. When Falnamuir came out of the hut Frann waved her towards us.

'Is your new baby a boy or a girl?'

'It's a boy.'

'And is he lovely? We're getting a new baby soon in the Round of Wood.'

Falnamuir reached down to brush some of Frann's hair from her eyes in a motherly way. 'When we're all settled down you can nurse him for a while. Would you like that?'

'If his mother doesn't mind.'

Falnamuir sighed, and left us, shaking her head.

'You see, Dinn Keene? I don't think they mean to do us any harm.'

So it seemed. Neither of us could see into the future. We had no way of knowing how the affair would end.

On the fifth day of our captivity I saw something that I had never seen before, and which I have never seen since. Let me say now that I, Dinn Keene, am glad that I only ever saw it once.

I was mending nets at the time, for the Lake-dwellers liked to keep my hands busy. Instead of a short strap round my ankle they had given me a longer one, and this extra length of freedom allowed me to reach the wattle fence. Now and then I tested its strength with great care, for Emman supervised my mending, and I knew that he would kill me if I tried to break away.

Presently I got tired of tying knots. Frann was away somewhere else with Falnamuir, so I amused myself by staring across the lake at the blue hills, and thinking how lovely it would be to stand under the waterfall with my Frann and Oscar. Then Leah came out of the hut with her baby in her arms. She rocked him gently as she came to the fence.

I was surprised to see her, for the girl seemed

to think of the daylight as a thing to be risked only in an emergency. She was mad, I think. Her mind belonged to the Otherworld.

She pitched the child over the fence into the lake. After the first splash, the baby floated. Leah seemed content for the lake to have him, and returned to the hut. It was as if she put him to bed for the night.

Perhaps I cried out – probably I did, seeing how the folds of the shawl soaked up water and spread out. I knew it must surely sink soon, taking the baby down with it. Meanwhile Ogue himself darted from the hut, bellowing like one who has just been stung.

'Here!' I shouted. 'It's in the water.'

The entire fence shook the whole way round as Ogue drove his body through it and hurled himself into the lake. With huge hands he seized the child, and with water lapping at his armpits, returned to the island and Falnamuir, who accepted the dripping bundle with outstretched arms. Then they all went into the hut.

Looking about me, I found myself alone except for the animals and two waifs sitting on the turf pile. Through the hole in the fence I saw islands dotted about the lake like sods of earth – at my feet the water lapped the rim of the Ducknest, this prison of mine. All I had to do was slip the thong at my ankle and I would be nearly at Thunder-oak before they knew I was gone. On the land they would never catch me.

But I could not leave without Frann. Even as I thought these things she appeared from the hut and hurried to the goatpost with misery in her face, where she tied herself up without a word.

'Frann, listen, there's nobody about. We could go now.'

A mighty shudder travelled through her. 'Did you see what she did? She threw it in the water, her own wee baby.'

'Frann …'

'Her own baby! They're beating her but she doesn't care.'

'Why did she do it?'

'I don't know, nobody knows. One of them said it was the curse. She's terrified of Corag Mor, they all are. It's awful in there. I don't want to talk about it, Dinn Keene.'

She curled up in a tight ball beside me, shivering, and wouldn't speak.

What a strange day in my life that was (said old Dinn Keene). Seen from afar, it has taken on the majesty of a mountain – neither good nor bad in itself, but awe-inspiring. I remember that I suddenly thought how that almost-drowned baby was the brother of Oscar. If the Lake-dwellers were right, then Ruadh was the father of them both. The business of living seemed more complicated than anyone had taught me to expect; and the truth, when it came out later, merely drove the lesson home.

By now it was too late to think of escaping, for Emman had come out with some others to stare through the hole in the fence, as if looking for reasons.

I thought of Corag Mor's curse, and felt that somehow I was part of it. We had to find a way of leaving this place.

PART FOUR

THE CROSS OF STONES

CHAPTER 11

I, Dinn Keene, can easily imagine how hard it was for Ard Bruill at this time.

Eithne told me afterwards how he would sit on the slope above the Round, watching the colour of morning spread through the clouds like the dyeing of a great fleece: thinking of his daughter, whom he loved; of the boy Dinn Keene, whom he was obliged to protect; of his people, whose pride had been so mangled in recent days; and of the bitter feud, how it boiled the blood so that nothing would cool it.

Eithne and Murta came to him from the Round of Wood, carrying their new daughter. No-one knew then that Eithne's child had been born on the same day as Leah's had been born in the Round of Water. If indeed there are beings who plan our lives, they play us some wonderful tricks.

'Bruill,' said Eithne, 'we want to be respectful. Murta and I are here to explain our intentions.'

'Intentions? How can you pair have intentions?'

'In case they cause trouble,' added Murta.

'Get on with it, then. Come into the queue!'

'It's about our baby,' said Eithne. 'We think she's in danger. Corag Mor says that Murta should not have chopped the Thunder-oak with the axe. It's possible that he may have caused offence and … well, as you know, the baby doesn't sleep. She's restless.'

'I took the decision to meddle with the tree. Go away and let me worry about it.'

'But Murta was the first one after you to make a cut.'

'What can *I* do about it?' Bruill asked Eithne, bluntly. 'Go to the Round of Stones and leave a ribbon there like anybody else.'

'We believe,' said Murta, 'that the Man of Speech can protect our daughter by putting water on her head.'

'Water? On her head?'

'And by talking to the God-all-Father and Mary's Great Son. He's told us how it works but

we are afraid that Corag Mor will come to you
and say things about us. Look, he's watching us
now.'

A glance confirmed this. The priest stood
motionless by the gate, staring up the hill. To see
him there somehow added to Bruill's sense of
foreboding. Recently Corag Mor had taken to
rejecting all meals but the first one of the day, and
he now wove twigs of ash and elder into his hair
so that it swooped above his head in loops and
whirls. No doubt he was gathering powers into
himself, thought Bruill; but the effect of these
things was to put more and more distance between himself and the others.

'Do what you like,' he said gruffly to Eithne and
Murta. 'On your own heads be it if the child
sickens. When you go back, tell the Man of
Speech I want to see him here.'

Ancell, thus summoned, duly came.

'This is a swamp we're in, Wanderer,' said
Bruill. 'I don't see how we can beat them by force,
so I'm going over to their Ducknest in the morning and I want you with me.'

'Why me? Why not one of the others – Corag
Mor, for example?'

'What kind of a sly question is that? You know

that Corag Mor is their particular enemy, they won't deal with him. But you – you look harmless. To be honest, I'm worried about Corag Mor.'

'Because he won't lift the curse?'

'Yes, that too. But he has drawn into himself these last few days, the bones are sharp in his face.'

'He is fasting. Making himself strong.'

'I know,' said Bruill. 'And you are the reason why, Wanderer. It will be some battle between you, when one looks half-starved and the other forgives his enemies. And where are the weapons in this battle, eh? If you ask me, you're two of a kind. Be ready in the morning at first light.'

That evening, Murta and Eithne knelt with the Man of Speech in the shallows of the lake – three silhouettes. The event was talked of for a long time afterwards. Ancell ran water from his hand over the head of the new baby, and named her after the special mother of the man who died on the cross of wood. He also wet the heads of Eithne and Murta.

Shortly after this the first garlands appeared on the Cross of Stones.

CHAPTER 12

As I slept in Ogue's hut with my arms loosely circling Frann, I dreamed of a great warrior who called himself my father. He stood in a chariot under Thunder-oak with shield-bearing men around him, and these had fine horses under them. He came, too, with well-armed men of foot and these had dogs of war straining at the leash. In my dream the leech-legs of Kingfrog Ogue trembled like tadpole-jelly.

I wakened to find that in real life, Dinn Keene was doing the trembling. Emman had me by the shoulder.

'Get up, both of you. Look alive.'

'What for?'

'You're wanted outside.'

My heart thumped in my ears like an alarm.

There was something different in his manner. Perhaps another attack was starting and I would hang upside-down again on the bottom of a boat.

'Get up when you're told!' he said again, shoving me at the door. Outside, in the morning's dazzle, I saw the Man of Speech standing there with Ard Bruill.

Had we been set free? Frann raced into her Daddy's arms and hung there until Dara took her to one side, saying, 'There, you've seen her. Now we can talk.'

Chairs of willow-reed came forward for Ogue and Ard Bruill; the rest of us made do with short logs. Falnamuir nursed Leah's baby while she listened to Bruill.

'Some of our people have said that I should come here and talk to you. Of course some were against it, but I agreed. Anyway, I'm here. I'm not sure what to say ...'

'Why did you come then?' asked Dara. And Falnamuir, furious with him, told him to hold his tongue.

'... except to say this: it is true that there is a dispute between us, it would be stupid to deny what we all know. But these children are not part of it. They came here of their own accord and I will punish them for it. I'm asking you to let them return with me now.'

'They will stay here until you accept our payment for Ruadh's life, and until Corag Mor lifts his curse.'

A flush came into Bruill's face, and seemed to make his words hot. 'You came in the night and killed the chief man of our people! You must have known – surely you realised – that we would ask a blood-price?'

'Ruadh had to die,' Ogue replied calmly, 'otherwise the glen was not safe for women to gather in. That's his child you see there. The chief man of your people was a dangerous goat and he is better dead.'

'I don't believe this! Bring me the girl.'

'No,' cried Dara.

'I'll get her,' Falnamuir said quickly.

The girl called Leah was brought out to stand trembling before the company. How that shifty glance of hers moved from face to face, as if seeking something friendly! Eventually it settled on the ground.

'You were abused by Ruadh?' Bruill began quietly.

'Yes.'

'While gathering?'

'Yes.'

'Describe him.'

'He was short. Not tall.'

'Where in the glen?'

'At the head of the glen.'

'And you were gathering – what? What were you gathering at the head of the glen?'

'I think it was sloes.'

'Was it a fair day? Did you cry out?'

'I … think so.'

'And for you,' said Bruill, with a terrible whispering lowness in his voice, 'for you Ruadh was killed, his family was killed, his frail old dogs were killed, on your account this war has started. And you're lying, aren't you?'

Leah shook her head and would not look up.

'Lies! I knew the man, knew him like my own self – by that honest man's dead bones I swear he was never the sort to abuse you in the yew glen or anywhere else. Lies, I say! Lies, lies!'

The girl sank to her knees, beaten down there, I do believe, by the power in Bruill's voice. Ancell took her elbow, and settled her on his log beside him.

Dara pointed at Ogue. 'What is going on here?

Why are you allowing this?'

'Dara,' said Falnamuir, so quiet and so cold, 'let her be questioned. Leah is my daughter, and I know that she has not yet told the whole truth.'

I, Dinn Keene, have seen animals in the hunt who are unable either to fight or to flee. The look in Leah's eyes was that of a young doe who has a spear in her side, and waits.

But Ancell had her by the hands. 'This child is so afraid that she can't say more than one word at a time. And yet you all sit in a circle round her, asking for the truth. Don't you understand? Only people who are certain of forgiveness will tell you all of the truth. And you cannot forgive, because you are like wild beasts. All of you!'

And he looked carefully at all of them, as if to lodge a portion of the blame with each in turn.

Of course this caused a silence, which Ancell continued to make use of. 'Leah, I forgive you. In the name of the God-all-Father I take away the guilt and the shame and the fear. I forgive you for whatever you have done, and for whatever has been done to you. I can do this because the God-all-Father, who sent me, loves you completely.'

Ogue of the Frogs, his wife Falnamuir, Dara

and Emman and Leah herself had never until this moment heard mention of the God-all-Father. Why then, I have often wondered, did they tolerate these words from the Man of Speech?

Perhaps he had the force of novelty. It is as well that the silence continued. We all heard the girl whisper.

'It wasn't Ruadh.'

This, if anything, left the silence more profound than before.

'Who was it, then?' asked Ogue.

'We ... We used to meet ... in the Round of Stones.'

She lowered her head again, but it was Falna-muir who spoke for her. 'It was Corag Mor.'

The girl cried out, and fled into the hut.

The weight of the truth, it seemed, had come down on the company like a fall of rocks. The Man of Speech, however, had not been dashed by it.

'May I speak?' he asked.

Ogue waved a hand, if as granting him the freedom to jump in the lake if he felt like it.

'I do not belong with you people, I was not born here. These hills are not mine, nor this lake. But the words I speak belong here. It is possible to live without greed, without spite, without casting blame, without plunder, without envy, without fear – but as people respecting one another in a great family as the God-all-Father commands us to do. These are new words and they give you a choice. You can send your people to the buzzards and the crows one by one, or you can hear the voice of Mary's Great Son of Peace. Have the strength, Ard Bruill, to accept the payment.'

Bruill had his face in the cool of his palms. At last he nodded. 'We'll accept the payment. But you must make no move against any of our people. That includes Corag Mor.'

'Agreed. But that man has surrounded us with totems like so many snares. When his curse is finally lifted you can have these two back.'

So Frann and I must spend some more time among the flies of Ogue's island. Bruill seemed about to speak, but the Man of Speech was first.

'Corag Mor will lift his curse, that will be attended to.'

'How?' asked Ogue.

'It will be done.'

Then Frann and Ard Bruill spoke their good-byes at the hurdle-gate. 'And who does your hair in plaits now?' I heard her sing out merrily.

It was an innocent little question. How it bruises me still, to remember.

CHAPTER 13

Within the Round of Wood, a war began. There were no weapons, none that any of us could see. Ancell and Corag Mor fought without ever coming together – they delivered invisible blows and suffered invisible wounds. Perhaps this explains why only one of them survived. With a cut that bleeds, you have some chance. A limb may come off, and still you may recover and go on your way with a blackthorn crutch. But how do you cure a man who withers from within?

This is what happened. When Ard Bruill returned from the Ducknest, he called the people around him. Even Breasal was obliged to leave her spinning, and join them. Corag Mor listened impassively to all that was said, apparently unmoved by the quick glances of those present. No-one blamed him publicly, either then or afterwards; and he himself showed no remorse.

Bruill said, 'There it is, that's the situation. I'm going to accept payment for Ruadh and make the best of it, so if anybody objects you'd better speak out now.'

No-one protested. Bodman Tar picked sourly at his teeth. 'All right,' Bruill continued. 'The other problem is that things will stay as they are unless Corag Mor lifts his curse. The Lake-dwellers were firm about that, it seems to hang over them. So … I'm asking you to do that, Corag Mor.'

I, Dinn Keene, can imagine to this day that headpiece of twigs above the dyed face.

'Ard Bruill knows that I cannot grant the impossible. He knows that once given, a curse must fall.'

'Then let it fall on me,' said Ancell. People made room for him as he walked forward. 'I say there is no curse. But if there is, I call it down on me. Let it fall where it can do no harm, for the God-all-Father protects me day and night. You will see that none of the powers you think you have will touch me, Corag Mor.'

As surely as some winds carry the threat of rain,

so there was meaning in the gaze which Corag Mor fixed on Ancell. He got up then, and left to continue his fast in the Round of Stones.

Except for Murta and Eithne, who believed in Mary's Son of the Miracles, nobody went near Ancell the following day. It was said that even Halfwolf made a circle while passing him. Ard Bruill watched him carefully, but the Wanderer did not appear to weaken.

Real rain came.

Not the warm mizzle of late summer, but rain that turned the Round of Wood into a mud-pool. The outdoor fire was abandoned, children were fetched in from the storm and only Halfwolf remained at his post.

All the same, Bruill put on his otter-skin coat and went out in the afternoon.

The hills ran with aspiring little rivers over his bare toes. At the rim of the hollow he hesitated, thinking that it was not his place to interfere. The rowan was bright with berries, the ribbons danced in the wind. Below, the stones of the Round cast no shadows. Corag Mor lay stretched out on the damp ground.

Bruill's path into the hollow took him close by the rude stone cross – a curious oddity if ever there was one! He noted carefully the ring of flowers around it. Mountain flowers. There were not many such blooms left, thought Bruill, someone had worked hard to pick those.

Before he entered the Round he took a small pouch from his belt. Corag Mor did not see him until Bruill placed a supporting arm round his neck and brought the pouch to his lips.

He wouldn't take the water. Bruill avoided the deep, vague eyes. 'Listen to me, Corag Mor, I must tell you. The Man of Speech is not changed. I don't want you to go on with this any longer.'

The head shook. Perhaps a natural shiver in the wet and cold.

'Wait for a better day,' said Bruill. 'It's best if you come home with me now. We'll soon dry you down and have you by a warm fire.'

'They visit me,' said Corag Mor.

His dyes had come loose in wet streaks; his face ran with an unearthly blend of colours.

'Corag Mor, I can only tell you what I see. Believe me, the truest mirror is the eye of an old friend. He has too much magic for you. The Wanderer is quiet within himself, his mind is still.

And if I go back without you now, it's the finish of you.'

Ard Bruill waited a while for some sign or comment, then retreated from the Round.

A voice close by said, 'What do you think of him?' and Bruill almost jumped out of his otter-skin.

It was the Wanderer.

'What are you doing here? Are you trying to finish me off, too?'

'Forgive me, I was watching. I don't want to force myself forward, but he's very ill.'

'Won't last the night.' Bruill glanced back at the glistening stones. Was this a victory for the Wanderer, he thought? Perhaps it would add Corag Mor's influence to what he already had. 'Did you speak to him?'

'Yes.'

'And?'

'I told him that he was not my enemy. I told him to believe, to ask for pardon, and that he would see God.'

'And he spat in your face.'

'No, he smiled.'

'You're a puzzle to me, Wanderer,' said Bruill. 'You have no child, you have no woman, you have no wealth. You have no home, you feed one mouth. You have nothing to lose, nothing to defend. What keeps you here with us?'

Then Ard Bruill turned for home in the driven rain.

PART FIVE

THE COLOUR
OF THE WIND

CHAPTER 14

I, Dinn Keene, say that I loved the daughter of Ard Bruill – I loved her well. This tender feeling grew throughout the period of our captivity.

Sometimes she made up stories to tell me as we sat at our goatpost. They were stories about birds and people and talking fish and a family of water rats who lived on the moon. In one of her stories there were two curlews who loved one another so much that in each other's company they discovered a new way of seeing: they saw the colour of the wind.

Frann said, 'Dinn Keene, you remember the night when we were on the shore of the lake together? Well, it wasn't quite dark, but almost. And you asked me a question, do you remember?'

'Yes.'

'You threw stones at Oscar and made him go away so that we could be alone, I saw you do it, Dinn Keene. You wanted me to come away with you if ever your father came and took you down to the plains.'

'I remember, what about it?'

'I gave you the wrong answer. I would go. If my father said yes, I would come with you, Dinn Keene. Are you pleased?'

Let me address you directly, Patrick of the Pens (said old Dinn Keene). If you are a wise man as they say you are, you will know what a great moment it is when you become important in another person's eyes. I would have exchanged the goodwill of all the gods, everywhere, for the real presence of my Frann. She was the sunlight on my path.

Tender feelings, I have found, cannot ever be confined to one person – these feelings spread, like smiles and yawns and sneezes. Even the Lake-dwellers appeared to me in a different colour: the new and mellow Dinn Keene came to like the woman Falnamuir, respected Ogue, pitied his mad daughter, and understood some of the reasons behind the dark rage of Dara. Yes indeed, she showed me the colour of the wind. So I was thinking the night I fell asleep after Ard Bruill's visit to the Ducknest.

I woke towards dawn, aware that something dangerous was happening. Everyone seemed to be awake, except for Frann beside me. The children in Ogue's hut pressed themselves against the walls like frightened animals. Falnamuir clutched the new baby, and Leah sat up in bed, half-naked and wild-eyed. All this I saw by the light of a dim rush lamp.

What was happening here? I didn't realise that Frann was the cause of it until she suddenly arched her back, and began to talk nonsense in her sleep.

And Leah pointed at her, crying out, 'She has the Babbling Mouth. Stop her, stop her!'

The hurdle-gate flew away from the entrance as Dara crawled through, bringing an axe with a stone blade.

'It's him!' screamed Leah. 'I see him in her eyes. He sent her to me, he sent her, he …'

She slumped over in a faint. Falnamuir caught her and laid her down gently while Ogue and Dara stared at my Frann.

They believed that Corag Mor, or something, was trying to reach them through her while she was asleep and unable to prevent it.

I, Dinn Keene, was more afraid than I have ever been. No doubt I was affected like everyone else by the panic of that stupid girl.

'Leave her alone,' I shouted, 'she's only sleeping.'

Frann's eyes opened. They were empty eyes with none of her true nature in them. Then she woke fully and gazed at us all in wonder.

Soon Leah sat up again, sobbing in a goatskin. 'It was *him*. I heard him using her voice!'

'You are a mad woman,' I cried out. 'You hear things that aren't there, she was only dreaming.'

'Put them outside,' said Ogue, 'they can't stay in here. We'll see what to do in the morning.'

I did not sleep when they returned us to the goatpost. Instead, I began to pick at the patch where they had mended the hole in the wattle fence. We had spent our last night in that place.

The sky began to grow pale. Through the ever-widening hole the outline of the islands became more distinct and the cries of the first birds became so loud that I could not imagine how anyone slept through them.

All the same, thought Dinn Keene, we are going this time.

I slid through the fence with Frann after me. We were both calm. The water did not feel cold, for I was shivering already. I pulled with my arms as if to draw the very bank closer to us both. An arrow hissed into the water as if it was hot, but I was on my feet now and in shallow water. And Frann? Was Frann still behind me? I heard the wild sound of her splashing and the thud of my heart's blood in my head. Nor did I stop when I reached Thunder-oak, but ran into the bushes before I turned, expecting to see her with me.

They had a boat in the water, I scarcely saw it. Frann was moving feebly. Her hair was on the water like a spreading shawl. I saw it plainly and the arrow that Dara had put into her.

Then I ran. My legs carried me along, Dinn Keene simply did their bidding. I think I had demons in my head that day, for it is certain that more than one voice came screaming out of me as I was carried through the rushes and the brakes.

How long I ran, who knows. At the head of the glen I saw Oscar, who looked for a moment as though he would run away – before he greeted me with shouts and a hug.

Oscar. Oscar, my friend, my true friend, go you to the Round of Wood and bring the Man of Speech to me here; say to no-one that you've seen me, and bring him quickly.

CHAPTER 15

Ancell brought her home in one of those light little boats with the leather hides. The Man of Speech was slightly built, and as he came up the slope with Frann in his arms he was inclined to stumble on a loose stone. Of course it did not really matter whether he fell, since Frann could no longer be hurt; and yet to those who were watching it seemed more important than ever that he should not let her drop. Then Ard Bruill walked through the gateway and took her in his powerful arms.

She lay for most of the day within the Round of Wood, her arms crossed under an open sky. Towards evening, Bruill ordered Breasal to wash and braid her hair, but she had hardly started when he ran forward to push her aside. He fixed her hair with his own hand.

Shortly after that, Ancell got down beside her in the position for talking to the God-all-Father. Bruill saw and came over.

'Get up.'

'But I thought …'

'Come away, Wanderer.'

Ancell rose to his feet. 'I just wanted to say some words over her.'

'What for? What can you say to help her where she is now?'

'The God-all-Father …'

'Failed!' Bruill sounded out the word, then spun away. The word seemed to fall like a blow on the Man of Speech, who followed after him.

'Wait. With respect, Ard Bruill – what do you mean "failed"?'

'What it says. Failed. He did not stop the arrow. The Curse fell on this innocent thing.'

'I must say this to you. What happened to your daughter had nothing to do with a Curse.'

Ard Bruill stopped outside the door of his hut. 'Wanderer, you will stop talking.'

'Please, one moment. This is what happens when there is a feud. It is the same in the next country, over that mountain, over that sea, it takes people over, becomes a thing apart – it selects its own victims and you have no control over it. See for yourself! You either stop it, or it kills at random. You, them, anybody!'

There happened to be leaning against the hut a young pine which was being sharpened to take its place in the wooden round. Ard Bruill raised it up and settled it on Ancell's left shoulder. And while he talked, he tapped with it.

'I am not listening, Wanderer, I am confused. I know about life, because I have lived. I don't know about death, it is a country I have never been to. Unlike you and Corag Mor – you are great travellers, the pair of you. It seems you have ways of making strange journeys and coming back, ways of knowing, ways of listening, you have your conversations with … well, who knows with what? Now it must be true that there are great secrets, I don't deny it. But what does Ard Bruill know about who makes rainbows? What does Ard Bruill know about where his daughter is? I only know she's not with me now.'

'She's with the One who made her,' said Ancell.

'It will be winter soon,' Ard Bruill went on, as if Ancell had not spoken. 'And that is not the time to be in the mountains. It gets cold. You should leave the Round of Wood with some sun on your back. Today. You should leave today. If I see you tomorrow …' he tapped with the pole '… I will split you like a log.'

'But I thought …'

'I am not listening, Wanderer. You will say no more.'

I, Dinn Keene, knew that the Man of Speech must be careful at this moment, or no power anywhere could save him from the cold, deep rage which had come over Ard Bruill in his loneliness. Ancell seemed to understand this, although he said, from a little way off, 'There will be others like me, my friend. Many of them.'

In the afternoon I walked into the hills, trying to snuff out all thought. I said to myself, Dinn Keene, you are Thunder-oak, a bolt has withered the best of your branches. I saw and heard the sweetness of her form and voice all around me, and had I known where memory lives within my body, I would have taken a knife to it.

Presently I came into the Round of Stones by way of Ulmar's Great Snare.

More horror waited for me here. I saw that the

Cross of Stones had been thrown down, and that the remains of Corag Mor lay under them, half-buried. His body had stiffened with the back arched and the head thrown back – the gaping mouth had already become a tunnel for inquisitive insects. Even his final act had been to destroy.

How I pitied that great and constant figure in my life now lying among the tumble of stones. How had he been with Leah when they met in their secret places? Which governed them – tenderness or terror? Or did it matter now?

I dragged him out and put him under a bush. After a fashion, I also rebuilt the Cross of Stones. And when I had finished the rebuilding, I cannot say that I understood it any more than I understood the Round of Stones. I wanted to believe that one was for the old way which had taken away my lovely Frann, and that the other might have saved her.

I knelt down, and listened. If ever anyone had been prepared to receive some small understanding of a great truth, it was I. But Dinn Keene heard only the soughing wind in the rowan tree.

CHAPTER 16

There is little more that I can say (said old Dinn Keene). I never saw Ancell again, or heard word of him, either. Eithne continued to speak of the Great Son of Mary the Maiden and kept a vigil of flowers at the stone cross in the hills.

As for Dinn Keene, Ard Bruill gave me respect, but not affection. He blamed me, I think, as indeed he blamed everyone, including himself, because the curse had fallen on his fair-haired daughter.

Before long the first frosts of winter made the heather brittle. One day a company of horsemen rode towards the Round of Wood from the direction of Bad Pig's Gap. They wore fine cloaks, fastened at the shoulder with sparkling brooches. My real father was not among them, but they had come to fetch Dinn Keene down to the plains again. One of the extra horses they had brought was only for me. My friend Oscar begged to come with me, but Ard Bruill would not allow it.

Within Ogue's Ducknest on the lake there cannot have been much room at that time of year if, like us, they had brought their animals in from the cold.

That morning – Falnamuir said afterwards – Ogue kicked down the hurdle of his hut and emerged with an armful of stale straw. His intention would have been, perhaps, to return with an armful of ice-hardened peat.

Glancing over the wattle fence, he saw the horseman on the ice.

As it happened, my father's warriors thought the ice was too risky to commit the horses, so they went forward on foot. Even as Ogue bellowed for Emman, Dara and the others, he knew that he had been careless that morning. He should have broken the ice.

There was resistance of a kind – time, even, to tip some hot ash on to the hissing ice. But by then the battleaxes were splitting through the weave of his nest and his people were unravelling with terror.

A black wind swept over the lake. I, Dinn

Keene, say that I sat mounted under the Thunder-oak, weeping for the want of Ard Bruill's daughter.

OTHER BOOKS FROM THE O'BRIEN PRESS

Classic Celtic Tales Series

THE HUNT FOR DIARMAID AND GRÁINNE

Liam Mac Uistin
Illustrated by Laura Cronin

A simple retelling of the great Celtic tale. Fionn loves Gráinne, but she loves the much younger Diarmaid and runs off with him, setting in train a series of tragic and stirring events. An exciting story of adventure, loyalty, love and fate.

Paperback £3.99/€5.07/$7.95

THE TÁIN

Liam Mac Uistin
Illustrated by Donald Teskey

The most famous Irish legend of all in an exciting and easily understood version. Tells of the great battle between the warrior Cúchulainn and his friend, Ferdia.

Paperback £3.99/€5.07/$7.95

CELTIC MAGIC TALES

Liam Mac Uistin
Illustrated by Maria A Negrin

The rich lore of magic from the ancient Celts fills these stories of the love quest of Mir and Aideen, the adventure of the sons of Tuireann, the mischievous Bricriu and the famous love epic of Deirdre.

Paperback £4.99/€6.34/$7.95

CELTIC TALES OF ENCHANTMENT

Liam Mac Uistin

More fabulous, memorable tales of Celtic times from this master storyteller.

Paperback £5.47/€6.95/$7.95

Send for our full colour catalogue

ORDER FORM

Please send me the books as marked.

I enclose cheque/postal order for £ . . . . (+£1.00 P&P per title)
OR please charge my credit card ☐ Access/Mastercard ☐ Visa

Card Number __ __ __ __   __ __ __ __   __ __ __ __   __ __ __ __

Expiry Date __ __/__ __

Name. . . . . Tel. . . . .

Address . . . .

. . . .

Please send orders to: THE O'BRIEN PRESS, 20 Victoria Road, Dublin 6.

Tel: +353 1 4923333; Fax: + 353 1 4922777; E-mail: books@obrien.ie

Website: www.obrien.ie

Note: prices are subject to change without notice